NUMBER PROPERTIES

Math Strategy Guide

This foundational guide provides a comprehensive analysis of the properties and rules of integers tested on the GMAT. Learn, practice, and master everything from prime products to perfect squares.

Number Properties GMAT Strategy Guide, Fourth Edition

10-digit International Standard Book Number: 0-9824238-4-5
13-digit International Standard Book Number: 978-0-9824238-4-4

Note: *GMAT, Graduate Management Admission Test, Graduate Management
Admission Council,* and *GMAC* are all registered trademarks of the Graduate
Management Admission Council which neither sponsors nor is affiliated in any way
with this product.

8 GUIDE INSTRUCTIONAL SERIES

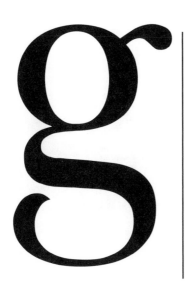

Math GMAT Strategy Guides

Number Properties (ISBN: 978-0-9824238-4-4)

Fractions, Decimals, & Percents (ISBN: 978-0-9824238-2-0)

Equations, Inequalities, & VICs (ISBN: 978-0-9824238-1-3)

Word Translations (ISBN: 978-0-9824238-7-5)

Geometry (ISBN: 978-0-9824238-3-7)

Verbal GMAT Strategy Guides

Critical Reasoning (ISBN: 978-0-9824238-0-6)

Reading Comprehension (ISBN: 978-0-9824238-5-1)

Sentence Correction (ISBN: 978-0-9824238-6-8)

ManhattanGMAT
the new standard

May 1st, 2009

Dear Student,

Thank you for picking up one of the Manhattan GMAT Strategy Guides—we hope that it refreshes your memory of the junior-high math that you haven't used in years. Maybe it will even teach you a new thing or two.

As with most accomplishments, there were many people involved in the various iterations of the book that you're holding. First and foremost is Zeke Vanderhoek, the founder of Manhattan GMAT. Zeke was a lone tutor in New York when he started the Company in 2000. Now, nine years later, MGMAT has Instructors and offices nationwide, and the Company contributes to the studies and successes of thousands of students each year.

Our 4th Edition Strategy Guides are based on the continuing experiences of our Instructors and our students. We owe much of these latest editions to the insight provided by our students. On the Company side, we are indebted to many of our Instructors, including but not limited to Josh Braslow, Dan Gonzalez, Mike Kim, Stacey Koprince, Ben Ku, Jadran Lee, David Mahler, Ron Purewal, Tate Shafer, Emily Sledge, and of course Chris Ryan, the Company's Lead Instructor and Director of Curriculum Development.

At Manhattan GMAT, we continually aspire to provide the best Instructors and resources possible. We hope that you'll find our dedication manifest in this book. If you have any comments or questions, please e-mail me at andrew.yang@manhattangmat.com. I'll be sure that your comments reach Chris and the rest of the team—and I'll read them too.

Best of luck in preparing for the GMAT!

Sincerely,

Andrew Yang
Chief Executive Officer
Manhattan GMAT

HOW TO ACCESS YOUR ONLINE RESOURCES

Please read this entire page of information, all the way down to the bottom of the page! This page describes WHAT online resources are included with the purchase of this book and HOW to access these resources.

If you are a registered Manhattan GMAT student and have received this book as part of your course materials, you have AUTOMATIC access to ALL of our online resources. This includes all practice exams, question banks, and online updates to this book. To access these resources, follow the instructions in the Welcome Guide provided to you at the start of your program. Do NOT follow the instructions below.

If you have purchased this book, your purchase includes 1 YEAR OF ONLINE ACCESS to the following:

> **6 Computer Adaptive Online Practice Exams**
>
> **Bonus Online Question Bank for *NUMBER PROPERTIES***
>
> **Online Updates to the Content in this Book**

ONLINE RESOURCE ACTIVATION

If you purchased this book from the Manhattan GMAT Online Store or at one of our Centers, you already have access to all practice exams and the Bonus Online Question Bank for *NUMBER PROPERTIES*. You can access them at **http://www.manhattangmat.com/practicecenter.cfm**. Otherwise, follow the instructions below.

To register and start using your online resources, please follow the instructions at the following URL:

http://www.manhattangmat.com/access.cfm   (Double check that you have typed this in accurately!)

Your one year of online access begins on the day that you register your book at the above URL. You only need to register your product ONCE at the above URL. To use your online resources any time AFTER you have completed the registration process, please login to the following URL:

http://www.manhattangmat.com/practicecenter.cfm

The 6 full-length computer adaptive practice exams included with the purchase of this book are delivered online using Manhattan GMAT's proprietary computer-adaptive test engine. The exams adapt to your ability level by drawing from a bank of more than 1,200 unique questions of varying difficulty levels written by Manhattan GMAT's expert instructors, all of whom have scored in the 99th percentile on the Official GMAT. At the end of each exam you will receive a score, an analysis of your results, and the opportunity to review detailed explanations for each question. You may choose to take the exams timed or untimed.

The Bonus Online Question Bank for *NUMBER PROPERTIES* consists of 25 extra practice questions (with detailed explanations) that test the variety of Number Properties concepts and skills covered in this book. These questions provide you with extra practice *beyond* the problem sets contained in this book. You may use our online timer to practice your pacing by setting time limits for each question in the bank.

The content presented in this book is updated periodically to ensure that it reflects the GMAT's most current trends. You may view all updates, including any known errors or changes, upon registering for online access.

Important Note: The 6 computer adaptive online exams included with the purchase of this book are the SAME exams that you receive upon purchasing ANY book in Manhattan GMAT's 8 Book Strategy Series. On the other hand, the Bonus Online Question Bank for *NUMBER PROPERTIES* is a unique resource that you receive ONLY with the purchase of this specific title.

PART I:
GENERAL

TABLE OF CONTENTS

g

PART II:
ADVANCED

TABLE OF CONTENTS

g

PART I: GENERAL

This part of the book covers both basic and intermediate topics within *Number Properties*. Complete Part I before moving on to Part II: Advanced.

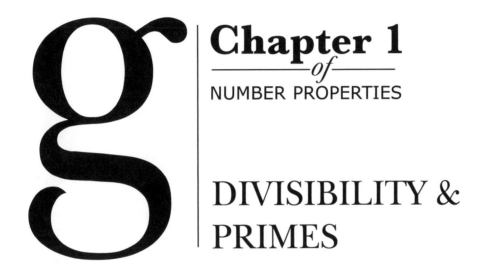

Chapter 1

of

NUMBER PROPERTIES

DIVISIBILITY & PRIMES

In This Chapter . . .

- Integers
- Arithmetic Rules
- Rules of Divisibility by Certain Integers
- Factors and Multiples
- Fewer Factors, More Multiples
- Divisibility and Addition/Subtraction
- Primes
- Prime Factorization
- Factor Foundation Rule
- The Prime Box
- Greatest Common Factor and Least Common Multiple
- Remainders

INTEGERS

Integers are "whole" numbers, such as 0, 1, 2, and 3, that have no fractional part. Integers can be positive (1, 2, 3...), negative (−1, −2, −3...), or the number 0.

The GMAT uses the term integer to mean a non-fraction or a non-decimal. The special properties of integers form the basis of most Number Properties problems on the GMAT.

Arithmetic Rules

Most arithmetic operations on integers will always result in an integer. For example:

$4 + 5 = 9$	$(−2) + 1 = −1$	The sum of two integers is always an integer.
$4 − 5 = −1$	$(−2) − (−3) = 1$	The difference of two integers is always an integer.
$4 × 5 = 20$	$(−2) × 3 = −6$	The product of two integers is always an integer.

However, division is different. Sometimes the result is an integer, and sometimes it is not:

$8 ÷ 2 = 4$, but $2 ÷ 8 = \dfrac{1}{4}$

$(−8) ÷ 4 = −2$, but $(−8) ÷ (−6) = \dfrac{4}{3}$

The result of dividing two integers is SOMETIMES an integer. (This result is called the **quotient**.)

An integer is said to be **divisible** by another number if the integer can be divided by that number with an integer result (meaning that there is no remainder).

For example, 21 is divisible by 3 because when 21 is divided by 3, an integer is the result ($21 ÷ 3 = 7$). However, 21 is not divisible by 4 because when 21 is divided by 4, a non-integer is the result ($21 ÷ 4 = 5.25$).

Alternatively, we can say that 21 is divisible by 3 because 21 divided by 3 yields 7 with zero remainder. On the other hand, 21 is not divisible by 4 because 21 divided by 4 yields 5 with a remainder of 1.

Here are some more examples:

$8 ÷ 2 = 4$	Therefore, 8 is divisible by 2.
	We can also say that 2 is a **divisor** or **factor** of 8.
$2 ÷ 8 = 0.25$	Therefore, 2 is NOT divisible by 8.
$(−6) ÷ 2 = −3$	Therefore, −6 is divisible by 2.
$(−6) ÷ (−4) = 1.5$	Therefore, −6 is NOT divisible by −4.

Rules of Divisibility by Certain Integers

The Divisibility Rules are important shortcuts to determine whether an integer is divisible by 2, 3, 4, 5, 6, 8, 9, and 10.

<u>An integer is divisible by:</u>

2 if the integer is EVEN.

12 is divisible by 2, but 13 is not. Integers that are divisible by 2 are called "even" and integers that are not are called "odd." You can tell whether a number is even by checking to see whether the units (ones) digit is 0, 2, 4, 6, or 8. Thus, 1,234,567 is odd, because 7 is odd, whereas 2,345,678 is even, because 8 is even.

3 if the SUM of the integer's DIGITS is divisible by 3.

72 is divisible by 3 because the sum of its digits is 9, which is divisible by 3. By contrast, 83 is not divisible by 3, because the sum of its digits is 11, which is not divisible by 3.

4 if the integer is divisible by 2 TWICE, or if the LAST TWO digits are divisible by 4.

28 is divisible by 4 because you can divide it by 2 twice and get an integer result (28 ÷ 2 = 14, and 14 ÷ 2 = 7). For larger numbers, check only the last two digits. For example, 23,456 is divisible by 4 because 56 is divisible by 4, but 25,678 is not divisible by 4 because 78 is not divisible by 4.

5 if the integer ends in 0 or 5.

75 and 80 are divisible by 5, but 77 and 83 are not.

6 if the integer is divisible by BOTH 2 and 3.

48 is divisible by 6 since it is divisible by 2 (it ends with an 8, which is even) AND by 3 (4 + 8 = 12, which is divisible by 3).

8 if the integer is divisible by 2 THREE TIMES, or if the LAST THREE digits are divisible by 8.

32 is divisible by 8 since you can divide it by 2 three times and get an integer result (32 ÷ 2 = 16, 16 ÷ 2 = 8, and 8 ÷ 2 = 4). For larger numbers, check only the last 3 digits. For example, 23,456 is divisible by 8 because 456 is divisible by 8, whereas 23,556 is not divisible by 8 because 556 is not divisible by 8.

9 if the SUM of the integer's DIGITS is divisible by 9.

4,185 is divisible by 9 since the sum of its digits is 18, which is divisible by 9. By contrast, 3,459 is not divisible by 9, because the sum of its digits is 21, which is not divisible by 9.

10 if the integer ends in 0.

670 is divisible by 10, but 675 is not.

The GMAT can also test these divisibility rules in reverse. For example, if you are told that a number has a ones digit equal to 0, you can infer that that number is divisible by 10. Similarly, if you are told that the sum of the digits of x is equal to 21, you can infer that x is divisible by 3 but NOT by 9.

Note also that there is no rule listed for divisibility by 7. The simplest way to check for divisibility by 7, or by any other number not found in this list, is to perform long division.

It is a good idea to memorize the rules for divisibility by 2, 3, 4, 5, 6, 8, 9 and 10.

*Manhattan*GMAT*Prep
the new standard

Factors and Multiples

Factors and Multiples are essentially opposite terms.

A **factor** is a positive integer that divides evenly into an integer. 1, 2, 4 and 8 are all the factors (also called divisors) of 8.

A **multiple** of an integer is formed by multiplying that integer by any integer, so 8, 16, 24, and 32 are some of the multiples of 8. Additionally, negative multiples are possible (–8, –16, –24, –32, etc.), but the GMAT does not test negative multiples directly. Also, zero (0) is technically a multiple of every number, because that number times zero (an integer) equals zero.

Note that an integer is always both a factor and a multiple of itself, and that 1 is a factor of every integer.

An easy way to find all the factors of a SMALL number is to use **factor pairs**. Factor pairs for any integer are the pairs of factors that, when multiplied together, yield that integer.

To find the factor pairs of a number such as 72, you should start with the automatic factors: 1 and 72 (the number itself). Then, simply "walk upwards" from 1, testing to see whether different numbers are factors of 72. Once you find a number that is a factor of 72, find its partner by dividing 72 by the factor. Keep walking upwards until all factors are exhausted.

Step by step:
(1) Make a table with 2 columns labeled "Small" and "Large."
(2) Start with 1 in the small column and 72 in the large column.
(3) Test the next possible factor of 72 (which is 2). 2 is a factor of 72, so write "2" underneath the "1" in your table. Divide 72 by 2 to find the factor pair: 72 ÷ 2 = 36. Write "36" in the large column.
(4) Test the next possible factor of 72 (which is 3). Repeat this process until the numbers in the small and the large columns run into each other. In this case, once we have tested 8 and found that 9 was its paired factor, we can stop.

Small	Large
1	72
2	36
3	24
4	18
6	12
8	9

You can use factor pairs to determine all of the factors of any integer, in theory, but the process works best with small numbers.

Fewer Factors, More Multiples

Sometimes it is easy to confuse factors and multiples. The mnemonic "Fewer Factors, More Multiples" should help you remember the difference. Factors divide into an integer and are therefore less than or equal to that integer. Positive multiples, on the other hand, multiply out from an integer and are therefore greater than or equal to that integer.

Any integer only has a limited number of factors. For example, there are only four factors of 8: 1, 2, 4, and 8. By contrast, there is an infinite number of multiples of an integer. For example, the first 5 positive multiples of 8 are 8, 16, 24, 32, and 40, but you could go on listing multiples of 8 forever.

Factors, multiples, and divisibility are very closely related concepts. For example, 3 is a factor of 12. This is the same as saying that 12 is a multiple of 3, or that 12 is divisible by 3.

multiple is the product

On the GMAT, this terminology is often used interchangeably in order to make the problem seem harder than it actually is. Be aware of the different ways that the GMAT can phrase information about divisibility. Moreover, try to convert all such statements to the same terminology. For example, **all** of the following statements **say exactly the same thing**:

- 12 is divisible by 3
- 12 is a multiple of 3
- $\dfrac{12}{3}$ is an integer
- $12 = 3n$, where n is an integer
- 12 items can be shared among 3 people so that each person has the same number of items.

- 3 is a divisor of 12, or 3 is a factor of 12
- 3 divides 12
- $\dfrac{12}{3}$ yields a remainder of 0
- 3 "goes into" 12 evenly

The GMAT can state that x is divisible by y in several different ways—learn these different phrasings and mentally convert them to a single form when you see them!

Divisibility and Addition/Subtraction

If you add two multiples of 7, you get another multiple of 7. Try it: $35 + 21 = 56$. This should make sense: $(5 \times 7) + (3 \times 7) = (5 + 3) \times 7 = 8 \times 7$.

Likewise, if you subtract two multiples of 7, you get another multiple of 7. Try it: $35 - 21 = 14$. Again, we can see why: $(5 \times 7) - (3 \times 7) = (5 - 3) \times 7 = 2 \times 7$.

This pattern holds true for the multiples of any integer N. **If you add or subtract multiples of N, the result is a multiple of N.** You can restate this principle using any of the disguises above: for instance, if N is a divisor of x and of y, then N is a divisor of $x + y$.

Primes

Prime numbers are a very important topic on the GMAT. A prime number is any positive integer larger than 1 with exactly two factors: 1 and itself. In other words, a prime number has NO factors other than 1 and itself. For example, 7 is prime because the only factors of 7 are 1 and 7. However, 8 is not prime because it is divisible by 2 and 4.

Note that the number 1 is not considered prime, as it has only one factor (itself). **Thus, the first prime number is 2, which is also the only even prime.** The first ten prime numbers are 2, 3, 5, 7, 11, 13, 17, 19, 23, and 29. You should memorize these primes.

Prime Factorization

One very helpful way to analyze a number is to break it down into its prime factors. This can be done by creating a prime factor tree, as shown to the right with the number 72. Simply test different numbers to see which ones "go into" 72 without leaving a remainder. Once you find such a number, then split 72 into factors. For example, 72 is divisible by 6, so it can be split into 6 and $72 \div 6$, or 12. Then repeat this process on the factors of 72 until every branch on the tree ends at a prime number. Once we only have primes, we stop, because we cannot split prime numbers into two smaller factors. In this example, 72 splits into 5 total prime factors (including repeats): $2 \times 3 \times 2 \times 2 \times 3$.

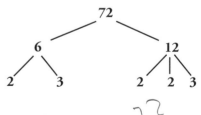

Prime factorization is an extremely important tool to use on the GMAT. One reason is that once we know the prime factors of a number, we can determine ALL the factors of that number, even large numbers. The factors can be found by building all the possible products of the prime factors.

On the GMAT, prime factorization is useful for many other applications in addition to enumerating factors. Some other situations in which you might need to use prime factorization include the following:

    (1) Determining whether one number is divisible by another number
    (2) Determining the greatest common factor of two numbers
    (3) Reducing fractions
    (4) Finding the least common multiple of two (or more) numbers
    (5) Simplifying square roots
    (6) Determining the exponent on one side of an equation with integer constraints

Prime numbers are the building blocks of integers. Many problems require variables to be integers, and you can often solve or simplify these problems by analyzing primes. A simple rule to remember is this: **if the problem states or assumes that a number is an integer, you MAY need to use prime factorization to solve the problem**.

> Think of the prime factors of an integer as that integer's "foundation," from which all factors of that number (except 1) can be built.

Factor Foundation Rule

The GMAT expects you to know the factor foundation rule: **if *a* is a factor of *b*, and *b* is a factor of *c*, then *a* is a factor of *c*.** In other words, any integer is divisible by all of its factors—and it is also divisible by all of the FACTORS of its factors.

For example, if 72 is divisible by 12, then 72 is also divisible by all the factors of 12 (1, 2, 3, 4, 6, and 12). Written another way, if 12 is a factor of 72, then all the factors of 12 are also factors of 72. The Factor Foundation Rule allows us to conceive of factors as building blocks in a foundation. 12 and 6 are factors, or building blocks, of 72 (because 12×6 builds 72).

The number 12, in turn, is built from its own factors; for example, 4×3 builds 12. Thus, if 12 is part of the foundation of 72 and 12 in turn rests on the foundation built by its prime factors (2, 2, and 3), then 72 is also built on the foundation of 2, 2, and 3.

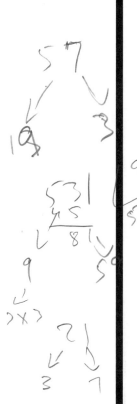

Going further, we can build almost any factor of 72 out of the bottom level of the foundation. For instance, we can see that 8 is a factor of 72, because we can build 8 out of the three 2's in the bottom row ($8 = 2 \times 2 \times 2$).

We say **almost** any factor, because one of the factors cannot be built out of the building blocks in the foundation: the number 1. Remember that the number 1 is not prime, but it is still a factor of every integer. Except for the number 1, every factor of 72 can be built out of the lowest level of 72 building blocks.

The Prime Box

The easiest way to work with the Factor Foundation Rule is with a tool called a Prime Box. A Prime Box is exactly what its name implies: a box that holds all the prime factors of a number (in other words, the lowest-level building blocks). Here are prime boxes for 72, 12, and 125:

72

| 2, 2, 2, 3, 3 |

12

| 2, 2, 3 |

125

| 5, 5, 5 |

Every integer larger than 1 has a unique prime factorization.

Notice that we must repeat copies of the prime factors if the number has multiple copies of that prime factor. You can use the prime box to test whether or not a specific number is a factor of another number.

Is 27 a factor of 72?

72

| 2, 2, 2, 3, 3 |

$27 = 3 \times 3 \times 3$. But we can see that 72 only has <u>two</u> 3's in its prime box. Therefore we cannot make 27 from the prime factors of 72. Thus, 27 is not a factor of 72.

Given that the integer n is divisible by 3, 7, and 11, what other numbers must be divisors of n?

n

| 3, 7, 11, ... ? |

Since we know that 3, 7, and 11 are prime factors of n, we know that n must also be divisible by all the possible **products** of the primes in the box: 21, 33, 77, and 231.

Without even knowing what n is, we have found 4 more of its factors: 21, 33, 77, and 231.

Notice also the ellipses and question mark ("... ?") in the prime box of n. This reminds us that we have created a **partial prime box** of n. Whereas the COMPLETE set of prime factors of 72 can be calculated and put into its prime box, we only have a PARTIAL list of prime factors of n, because n is an unknown number. We know that n is divisible by 3, 7, and 11, but we do NOT know what additional primes, if any, n has in its prime box.

Most of the time, when building a prime box for a VARIABLE, we will use a partial prime box, but when building a prime box for a NUMBER, we will use a complete prime box.

*Manhattan*GMAT*Prep
the new standard

Greatest Common Factor and Least Common Multiple

Frequently on the GMAT, you may have to find the Greatest Common Factor (GCF) or Least Common Multiple (LCM) of a set of two or more numbers.

> **Greatest Common Factor (GCF):** the largest divisor of two or more integers.
> **Least Common Multiple (LCM):** the smallest multiple of two or more integers.

It is likely that you already know how to find both the GCF and the LCM. For example, when you reduce the fraction $\frac{9}{12}$ to $\frac{3}{4}$, you are dividing both the numerator (9) and denominator (12) by 3, which is the GCF of 9 and 12. When you add together the fractions $\frac{1}{2} + \frac{1}{3} + \frac{1}{5}$, you convert the fractions to thirtieths: $\frac{1}{2} + \frac{1}{3} + \frac{1}{5} = \frac{15}{30} + \frac{10}{30} + \frac{6}{30} = \frac{31}{30}$.

Why thirtieths? The reason is that 30 is the LCM of the denominators: 2, 3, and 5.

The GCF and the LCM can best be understood visually by using a Venn diagram.

FINDING GCF AND LCM USING VENN DIAGRAMS

One way that you can visualize the GCF and LCM of two numbers is by placing prime factors into a **Venn diagram**—a diagram of circles showing the overlapping and non-overlapping elements of two sets. To find the GCF and LCM of two numbers using a Venn diagram, perform the following steps:

(1) Factor the numbers into primes.
(2) Create a Venn diagram.
(3) Place each common factor, including copies of common factors appearing more than once, into the shared area of the diagram (the shaded region to the right).
(4) Place the remaining (non-common) factors into the non-shared areas.

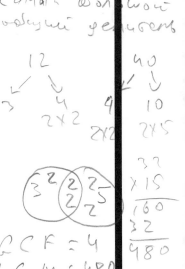

The Venn diagram above illustrates how to determine the GCF and LCM of 30 and 24. **The GCF is the product of primes in the overlapping region**: $2 \times 3 = 6$. **The LCM is the product of ALL primes in the diagram**: $5 \times 2 \times 3 \times 2 \times 2 = 120$.

Compute the GCF and LCM of 12 and 40 using the Venn diagram approach.

The prime factorizations of 12 and 40 are $2 \times 2 \times 3$ and $2 \times 2 \times 2 \times 5$, respectively:

The only common factors of 12 and 40 are two 2's. Therefore, we place two 2's in the shared area of the Venn diagram (on the next page) and remove them from BOTH prime factorizations. Then, place the remaining factors in the zones belonging exclusively to 12 and 40. These two outer regions **must have *no* primes in common!**

12	40
2, 2, 3	2, 2, 2, 5

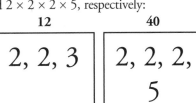

The GCF of 12 and 40 is therefore $2 \times 2 = 4$, the product of the primes in the **shared area**. (An easy way to remember this is that the "common factors" are in the "common area.")

The LCM is $2 \times 2 \times 2 \times 3 \times 5 = 120$, the product of **all** the primes in the diagram.

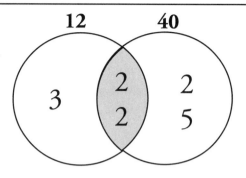

The product of the shared primes is the GCF. The product of all the primes (counting shared primes just once) is the LCM.

Note that if two numbers have NO primes in common, then their GCF is 1 and their LCM is simply their product. For example, 35 (= 5×7) and 6 (= 2×3) have no prime numbers in common. Therefore, their GCF is 1 (the common factor of *all* positive integers) and their LCM is $35 \times 6 = 210$. Be careful: even though you have no primes in the common area, the GCF is not 0 but 1.

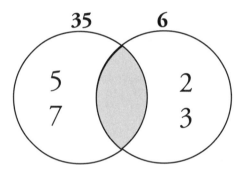

Remainders

The number 17 is not divisible by 5. When you divide 17 by 5, using long division, you get a **remainder:** a number left over. In this case, the remainder is 2.

$$
\begin{array}{r}
3 \\
5)\overline{17} \\
-15 \\
\hline
2
\end{array}
$$

We can also write that 17 is 2 more than 15, or 2 more than a multiple of 5. In other words, we can write $17 = 15 + 2 = 3 \times 5 + 2$. Every number that leaves a remainder of 2 after it is divided by 5 can be written this way: as a multiple of 5, plus 2.

On simpler remainder problems, it is often easiest to pick numbers. Simply add the desired remainder to a multiple of the divisor. For instance, if you need a number that leaves a remainder of 4 after division by 7, first pick a multiple of 7: say, 14. Then add 4 to get 18, which satisfies the requirement ($18 = 7 \times 2 + 4$).

Problem Set

For problems #1–12, use one or more prime boxes, if appropriate, to answer each question: YES, NO, or CANNOT BE DETERMINED. If your answer is CANNOT BE DETERMINED, use two numerical examples to show how the problem could go either way. All variables in problems #1 through #12 are assumed to be integers unless otherwise indicated.

1. If a is divided by 7 or by 18, an integer results. Is $\dfrac{a}{42}$ an integer?

2. If 80 is a factor of r, is 15 a factor of r?

3. Given that 7 is a factor of n and 7 is a factor of p, is $n + p$ divisible by 7?

4. Given that 8 is not a factor of g, is 8 a factor of $2g$?

5. If j is divisible by 12 and 10, is j divisible by 24?

6. If 12 is a factor of xyz, is 12 a factor of xy?

7. Given that 6 is a divisor of r and r is a factor of s, is 6 a factor of s?

8. If 24 is a factor of h and 28 is a factor of k, must 21 be a factor of hk?

9. If 6 is not a factor of d, is $12d$ divisible by 6?

10. If k is divisible by 6 and $3k$ is not divisible by 5, is k divisible by 10?

11. If 60 is a factor of u, is 18 a factor of u?

12. If s is a multiple of 12 and t is a multiple of 12, is $7s + 5t$ a multiple of 12?

Solve Problems #13–15:

13. What is the greatest common factor of 420 and 660?

14. What is the least common multiple of 18 and 24?

15. A skeet shooting competition awards prizes as follows: the first place winner receives 11 points, the second place winner receives 7 points, the third place finisher receives 5 points, and the fourth place finisher receives 2 points. No other prizes are awarded. John competes in the skeet shooting competition several times and receives points every time he competes. If the product of all of the points he receives equals 84,700, how many times does he participate in the competition?

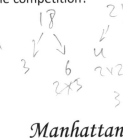

1. **YES:**

a

$$\boxed{2, 3, 3, 7, \ldots ?}$$

If *a* is divisible by 7 and by 18, its prime factors include 2, 3, 3, and 7, as indicated by the prime box to the left. Therefore, any integer that can be constructed as a product of any of these prime factors is also a factor of *a*. $42 = 2 \times 3 \times 7$. Therefore, 42 is also a factor of *a*.

2. **CANNOT BE DETERMINED:**

r

$$\boxed{2, 2, 2, 2, 5, \ldots ?}$$

If *r* is divisible by 80, its prime factors include 2, 2, 2, 2, and 5, as indicated by the prime box to the left. Therefore, any integer that can be constructed as a product of any of these prime factors is also a factor of *r*. $15 = 3 \times 5$. Since the prime factor 3 is not in the prime box, we cannot determine whether 15 is a factor of *r*. As numerical examples, we could take $r = 80$, in which case 15 is NOT a factor of *r*, or $r = 240$, in which case 15 IS a factor of *r*.

3. **YES:** If 2 numbers are both multiples of the same number, then their SUM is also a multiple of that same number. Since *n* and *p* share the common factor 7, the sum of *n* and *p* must also be divisible by 7.

4. **CANNOT BE DETERMINED:**

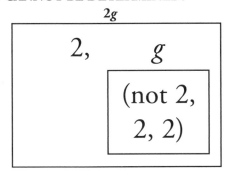

In order for 8 to be a factor of 2*g*, we would need two more 2's in the prime box. By the Factor Foundation Rule, *g* would need to be divisible by 4. We know that *g* is not divisible by 8, but there are certainly integers that are divisible by 4 and not by 8, such as 4, 12, 20, 28, etc. However, while we cannot conclude that *g* is **not** divisible by 4, we cannot be certain that *g* **is** divisible by 4, either. As numerical examples, we could take $g = 5$, in which case 8 is NOT a factor of 2*g*, or $g = 4$, in which case 8 IS a factor of 2*g*.

5. **CANNOT BE DETERMINED:**

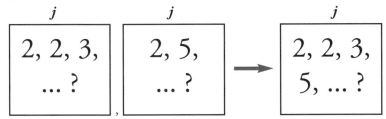

If *j* is divisible by 12 and by 10, its prime factors include 2, 2, 3, and 5, as indicated by the prime box to the left. There are only TWO 2's that are definitely in the prime factorization of *j*, because the 2 in the prime factorization of 10 may be REDUNDANT—that is, it may be the SAME 2 as one of the 2's in the prime factorization of 12.

$24 = 2 \times 2 \times 2 \times 3$. There are only two 2's in the prime box of *j*; 24 requires three 2's. Therefore, 24 is not necessarily a factor of *j*.

As another way to prove that we cannot determine whether 24 is a factor of *j*, consider 60. The number 60 is divisible by both 12 and 10. However, it is NOT divisible by 24. Therefore, *j* could equal 60, in which case it is not divisible by 24. Alternatively, *j* could equal 120, in which case it IS divisible by 24.

6. **CANNOT BE DETERMINED:**

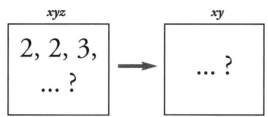

If *xyz* is divisible by 12, its prime factors include 2, 2, and 3, as indicated by the prime box to the left. Those prime factors could all be factors of *x* and *y*, in which case 12 is a factor of *xy*. For example, this is the case when $x = 20$, $y = 3$, and $z = 7$. However, *x* and *y* could be prime or otherwise not divisible by 2, 2, and 3, in which case *xy* is not divisible by 12. For example, this is the case when $x = 5$, $y = 11$, and $z = 24$.

7. **YES:** By the Factor Foundation Rule, if 6 is a factor of *r* and *r* is a factor of *s*, then 6 is a factor of *s*.

8. **YES:**

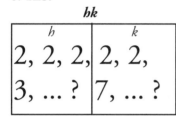

By the Factor Foundation Rule, all the factors of both *h* and *k* must be factors of the product, *hk*. Therefore, the factors of *hk* include 2, 2, 2, 2, 2, 3, and 7, as shown in the combined prime box to the left. $21 = 3 \times 7$. Both 3 and 7 are in the prime box. Therefore, 21 is a factor of *hk*.

9. **YES:**

12d

12	d
2, 2, 3	not 2 / not 3

The fact that *d* is not divisible by 6 is irrelevant in this case. Since 12 is divisible by 6, 12*d* is also divisible by 6.

10. **NO:**

3k

3	k
3	2, 3 / not 5

We know that 3*k* is not divisible by 5. Since 5 is prime, and 3 is not divisible by 5, we can conclude that *k* is not divisible by 5. If *k* is not divisible by 5, it cannot be divisible by 10, because 10 has a 2 and a 5 in its prime factorization.

11. **CANNOT BE DETERMINED:**

u

2, 2, 3, 5, ... ?

If *u* is divisible by 60, its prime factors include 2, 2, 3, and 5, as indicated by the prime box to the left. Therefore, any integer that can be constructed as a product of any of these prime factors is also a factor of *u*. $18 = 2 \times 3 \times 3$. Since there is only one 3 in the prime box, we cannot determine whether or not 18 is a factor of *u*. As numerical examples, we could take $u = 60$, in which case 18 is NOT a factor of *u*, or $u = 180$, in which case 18 IS a factor of *u*.

12. **Yes:**
If *s* is a multiple of *t*, then so is 7*s*
If *t* is a multiple of 12, then so is 5*t*.
Since 7*s* and 5*t* are both multiples of 12, then their *sum* (7*s* + 5*t*) is also a multiple of 12.

13. **60:**

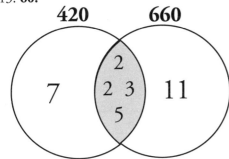

$420 = 2 \times 2 \times 3 \times 5 \times 7$.
$660 = 2 \times 2 \times 3 \times 5 \times 11$.
The greatest common factor is the product of the primes in the shared factors ONLY:
$2^2 \times 3^1 \times 5^1 = 2 \times 2 \times 3 \times 5 = 60$.

14. **72:**

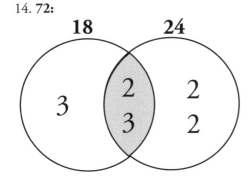

$18 = 2 \times 3 \times 3$.
$24 = 2 \times 2 \times 2 \times 3$.
The least common multiple is the product of all the primes in the diagram:
$3 \times 2 \times 3 \times 2 \times 2 = 72$.

15. **7:** Notice that the values for scoring first, second, third, and fourth place in the competition are all prime numbers. Notice also that the PRODUCT of all of the scores John received is known. Therefore, if we simply take the prime factorization of the product of his scores, we can determine what scores he received (and how many scores he received).

$84{,}700 = 847 \times 100 = 7 \times 121 \times 2 \times 2 \times 5 \times 5 = 7 \times 11 \times 11 \times 2 \times 2 \times 5 \times 5$.

Thus John received first place twice (11 points each), second place once (7 points each), third place twice (5 points each), and fourth place twice (2 points each.) He received a prize 7 times, so he competed 7 times.

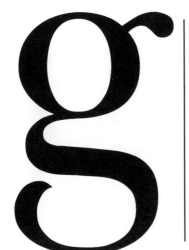

Chapter 2
of
NUMBER PROPERTIES

ODDS & EVENS

In This Chapter . . .

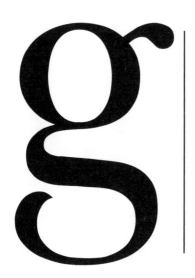

- Arithmetic Rules of Odds & Evens
- The Sum of Two Primes
- Testing Odd & Even Cases

ODDS & EVENS

Even numbers are integers that are divisible by 2. Odd numbers are integers that are not divisible by 2. All integers are either even or odd.

Evens: 0, 2, 4, 6, 8, 10, 12…   Odds: 1, 3, 5, 7, 9, 11…

Consecutive integers alternate between even and odd: 9, 10, 11, 12, 13…
                                                         O, E, O, E, O…

Negative integers are also either even or odd:

Evens: −2, −4, −6, −8, −10, −12…   Odds: −1, −3, −5, −7, −9, −11…

Arithmetic Rules of Odds & Evens

The GMAT tests your knowledge of how odd and even numbers combine through addition, subtraction, multiplication, and division. Rules for adding, subtracting, multiplying and dividing odd and even numbers can be derived by simply picking numbers and testing them out. While this is certainly a valid strategy, it also pays to memorize the following rules for operating with odds and evens, as they are extremely useful for certain GMAT math questions.

Addition and Subtraction:
Add or subtract 2 odds or 2 evens, and the result is EVEN.   7 + 11 = 18 and 8 + 6 = 14
Add or subtract an odd with an even, and the result is ODD.   7 + 8 = 15

Multiplication:
When you multiply integers, if ANY of the integers is $3 \times 8 \times 9 \times 13 = 2,808$
even, the result is EVEN.
Likewise, if NONE of the integers is even, then the result is ODD.

If you multiply together several even integers, the result will be divisible by higher and higher powers of 2. This result should make sense from our discussion of prime factors. Each even number will contribute at least one 2 to the factors of the product.

For example, if there are TWO even integers in a set of integers being multiplied together, the result will be divisible by 4. $2 \times 5 \times 6 = 60$ (divisible by 4)

If there are THREE even integers in a set of integers being multipled together, the result will be divisible by 8. $2 \times 5 \times 6 \times 10 = 600$ (divisible by 8)

To summarize so far:

Odd ± Even = ODD   Odd × Odd = ODD
Odd ± Odd = EVEN   Even × Even = EVEN (and divisible by 4)
Even ± Even = EVEN   Odd × Even = EVEN

If you forget these rules, you can always figure them out on the test by picking real numbers.

ODDS & EVENS STRATEGY

Division:

There are no guaranteed outcomes in division, because the division of two integers may not yield an integer result. There are several potential outcomes, depending upon the value of the dividend and divisor.

Divisibility of Odds & Evens

	Even?	**Odd?**	**Non-Integer?**
Even ÷ Even	✓ Example: $12 \div 2 = 6$	✓ Example: $12 \div 4 = 3$	✓ Example: $12 \div 8 = 1.5$
Even ÷ Odd	✓ Example: $12 \div 3 = 4$	✗	✓ Example: $12 \div 5 = 2.4$
Odd ÷ Even	✗	✗	✓ Example: $9 \div 6 = 1.5$
Odd ÷ Odd	✗	✓ Example: $15 \div 5 = 3$	✓ Example: $15 \div 25 = 0.6$

An odd number divided by any other integer CANNOT produce an even integer. Also, an odd number divided by an even number CANNOT produce an integer, because the odd number will never be divisible by the factor of 2 concealed within the even number.

The Sum of Two Primes

Notice that all prime numbers are odd, except the number 2. (All larger even numbers are divisible by 2, so they cannot be prime.) Thus, the sum of any two primes will be even ("Add two odds . . ."), unless one of those primes is the number 2. So, if you see a sum of two primes that is odd, one of those primes must be the number 2. Conversely, if you know that 2 CANNOT be one of the primes in the sum, then the sum of the two primes must be even.

> If *a* and *b* are both prime numbers greater than 10, which of the following CANNOT be true?
>
> I. *ab* is an even number.
> II. The difference between *a* and *b* equals 117.
> III. The sum of *a* and *b* is even.
>
> (A) I only
> (B) I and II only
> (C) I and III only
> (D) II and III only
> (E) I, II and III

Remember that 2 is the ONLY even prime number.

Since a and b are both prime numbers greater than 10, they must both be odd. Therefore ab must be an odd number, so Statement I cannot be true. Similarly, if a and b are both odd, then $a - b$ cannot equal 117 (an odd number). This difference must be even. Therefore, Statement II cannot be true. Finally, since a and b are both odd, $a + b$ must be even, so Statement III will always be true. Since Statements I and II CANNOT be true, but Statement III IS true, the correct answer is (**B**).

Try the following Data Sufficiency problem. (If you are not familiar at all with the Data Sufficiency format, see pages 267–270 of the *Official Guide for GMAT Review, 12th edition*. You may also refer to Chapter 8 of this guide, "Strategies for Data Sufficiency.")

> If $x > 1$, what is the value of integer x?
>
> (1) There are x unique factors of x.
> (2) The sum of x and any prime number larger than x is odd.

Remember, you can always just test numbers to make sense of a statement such as "There are x unique factors of x."

Statement (1) tells us that there are x unique factors of x. In order for this to be true, EVERY integer between 1 and x, inclusive, must be a factor of x. Testing numbers, we can see that this property holds for 1 and for 2, but not for 3 or for 4. In fact, this property does not hold for any higher integer, because no integer x above 2 is divisible by $x - 1$. Therefore, $x = 1$ or 2. However, the original problem stem told us that $x > 1$, so x must equal 2. SUFFICIENT.

Statement (2) tells us that x plus any prime number larger than x is odd. Since $x > 1$, x must equal at least 2, so this includes only prime numbers larger than 2. Therefore, the prime number is odd, and x is even. However, this does not tell us which even number x could be. INSUFFICIENT. The correct answer is (**A**): Statement (1) is sufficient to answer the question, but Statement (2) is insufficient.

Testing Odd & Even Cases

Sometimes multiple variables can be odd or even, and you need to determine the implications of each possible scenario. In that case, set up a table listing all the possible odd/even combinations of the variables, and determine what effect that would have on the question.

> If a, b, and c are integers and $ab + c$ is odd, which of the following must be true?
>
> I. $a + c$ is odd
> II. $b + c$ is odd
> III. abc is even
>
> (A) I only
> (B) II only
> (C) III only
> (D) I and III only
> (E) II and III only

Here, a, b and c could all possibly be odd or even. Some combinations of Odds & Evens for a, b and c will lead to an odd result. Other combinations will lead to an even result. We need to test each possible combination to see what the result will be for each. Set up a table, as on the next page, and fill in the possibilities.

Scenario	*a*	*b*	*c*	*ab + c*
1	ODD	ODD	ODD	O × O + O = E
2	**ODD**	**ODD**	**EVEN**	**O × O + E = O**
3	**ODD**	**EVEN**	**ODD**	**O × E + O = O**
4	ODD	EVEN	EVEN	O × E + E = E
5	**EVEN**	**ODD**	**ODD**	**E × O + O = O**
6	EVEN	ODD	EVEN	E × O + E = E
7	**EVEN**	**EVEN**	**ODD**	**E × E + O = O**
8	EVEN	EVEN	EVEN	E × E + E = E

Scenarios 2, 3, 5 and 7 yield an odd result, and so we must focus only on those scenarios. We can conclude that Statement I is false (Scenario 3 yields $a + c$ = EVEN), Statement II is false (Scenario 5 yields $b + c$ = EVEN), and Statement III is true (all 4 working scenarios yield abc = EVEN). Therefore, the correct answer is (**C**).

When approaching Odds & Evens questions involving multiple variables, test different Odd/Even cases for each variable.

Problem Set

For questions #1–15, answer each question ODD, EVEN, or CANNOT BE DETERMINED. Try to explain each answer using the rules you learned in this section. All variables in problems #1–15 are assumed to be integers unless otherwise indicated.

1.   If n is odd, p is even, and q is odd, what is $n + p + q$?   ~Even~

2.   If r is a prime number greater than 2, and s is odd, what is rs?   Odd

3.   If t is odd, what is t^4?   odd $O \times O = O \times O = O \times O = O$

4.   If u is even and w is odd, what is $u + uw$? $e + e \times o = even$

5.   If $x \div y$ yields an odd integer, what is x? $\frac{x}{y} = odd$ CBD $\frac{12}{4} = 3$ $\frac{27}{3} = 9$

6.   If $a + b$ is even, what is ab? $O + O$ $O \times O = O$ CBD
                                            $e + e$ $e \times e = E$

7.   If c, d, and e are consecutive integers, what is cde?
       $e + O - I$ $O + O$ $O + e$ $3 \times 4 \times 5 = 60$ Even

8.   If f and g are prime numbers, what is $f + g$? CBD $2 \times 3 \times 4 = 24$

9.   If h is even, j is odd, and k is odd, what is $k(h + j)$? CBD $O + O = $ or $e + o$
                                                                       E   O

10.   If m is odd, what is $m^2 + m$? $=$ Even $2 + 3 + 4 + 5 = ev.$

11.   If n, p, q, and r are consecutive integers, what is their sum? Even $e + o + e + o$
                                                                              $o + e + o + e$
12.   If $t = s - 3$, what is $s + t$? Odd $3 + 4 + 5 + 6 = ev.$
                                                                              O   O
13.   If u is odd and w is even, what is $(uw)^2 + u$? Odd $s + s - 3 = odd$

14.   If xy is even and z is even, what is $x + z$? CBD

15.   If a, b, and c are consecutive integers, what is $a + b + c$? Odd

       $xy = even$ $e e$
                                                          $e o$
                                                          $o e$

$(O \times E)^2 + O = $ $e + o + e = odd$
                            $o + e + o$

$O(e + o) = $

1. **EVEN:** O + E = O. O + O = E. If in doubt, try plugging in actual numbers: 7 + 2 + 3 = 12 (even).

2. **ODD:** O × O = O. If in doubt, try plugging in actual numbers: 3 × 5 = 15 (odd).

3. **ODD:** O × O × O × O = O. If in doubt, try plugging in actual numbers: 3 × 3 × 3 × 3 = 81 (odd).

4. **EVEN:** *uw* is even. Therefore, E + E = E.

5. **CANNOT BE DETERMINED:** There are no guaranteed outcomes in division.

6. **CANNOT BE DETERMINED:** If *a* + *b* is even, *a* and *b* are either both odd or both even. If they are both odd, *ab* is odd. If they are both even, *ab* is even.

7. **EVEN:** At least one of the consecutive integers, *c*, *d*, and *e*, must be even. Therefore, the product *cde* must be even.

8. **CANNOT BE DETERMINED:** If either *f* or *g* is 2, then *f* + *g* will be odd. If *f* and *g* are odd primes, or if *f* and *g* are both 2, then *f* + *g* will be even.

9. **ODD:** *h* + *j* must be odd (E + O = O). Therefore, *k*(*h* + *j*) must be odd (O × O = O).

10. **EVEN:** m^2 must be odd (O × O = O). $m^2 + m$, therefore, must be even (O + O = E).

11. **EVEN:** If *n*, *p*, *q*, and *r* are consecutive integers, two of them must be odd and two of them must be even. You can pair them up to add them: O + O = E, and E + E = E. Adding the pairs, you will see that the sum must be even: E + E = E.

12. **ODD:** If *s* is even, then *t* must be odd. If *s* is odd, then *t* must be even. Either way, the sum must be odd: E + O = O, or O + E = O. (Try plugging in real numbers: if *s* = 2, *t* = 5, or if *s* = 3, *t* = 6.)

13. **ODD:** $(uw)^2$ must be even. Therefore, E + O = O.

14. **CANNOT BE DETERMINED:** If *xy* is even, then either *x* or *y* (or both *x* and *y*) must be even. Given that *z* is even, *x* + *z* could be O + E or E + E. Therefore, we cannot determine whether *x* + *z* is odd or even.

15. **CANNOT BE DETERMINED:** If *a*, *b*, and *c* are consecutive, then there could be either one or two even integers in the set. *a* + *b* + *c* could be O + E + O or E + O + E. In the first case, the sum is even; in the second, the sum is odd.

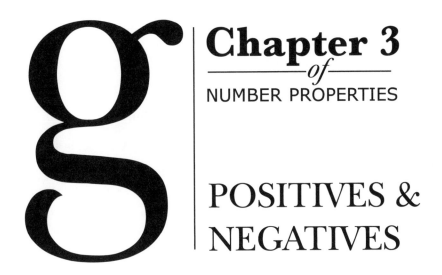

Chapter 3
of
NUMBER PROPERTIES

POSITIVES &
NEGATIVES

In This Chapter . . .

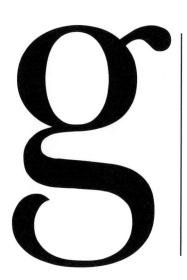

- Absolute Value: Absolutely Positive
- A Double Negative = A Positive
- Multiplying & Dividing Signed Numbers
- Testing Positive & Negative Cases
- Disguised Positive & Negative Questions

POSITIVES & NEGATIVES

Numbers can be either positive or negative (except the number 0, which is neither). A number line illustrates this idea:

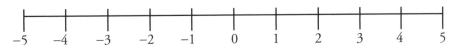

Negative numbers are all to the left of zero. Positive numbers are all to the right of zero.

Note that a variable (such as x) can have either a positive or a negative value, unless there is evidence otherwise. The variable x is not necessarily positive, nor is $-x$ necessarily negative.

Absolute Value: Absolutely Positive

The absolute value of a number answers this question: **How far away is the number from 0 on the number line?** For example, the number 5 is exactly 5 units away from 0, so the absolute value of 5 equals 5. Mathematically, we write this using the symbol for absolute value: $|5| = 5$. To find the absolute value of -5, look at the number line above: -5 is also exactly 5 units away from 0. Thus, the absolute value of -5 equals 5, or, in mathematical symbols, $|-5| = 5$. Notice that absolute value is always positive, because it disregards the direction (positive or negative) from which the number approaches 0 on the number line. When you interpret a number in an absolute value sign, just think: Absolutely Positive! (Except, of course, for 0, because $|0| = 0$, which is the smallest possible absolute value.)

On the number line above, note that 5 and -5 are the same distance from 0, which is located halfway between them. In general, if two numbers are opposites of each other, then they have the same absolute value, and 0 is halfway between. If $x = -y$, then we have either

(We cannot tell which variable is positive without more information.

A Double Negative = A Positive

A double negative occurs when a minus sign is in front of a negative number (which already has its own negative sign). For example:

What is $7 - (-3)$?

Just as you learned in English class, two negatives yield a positive:

$7 - (-3) = 7 + 3 = 10$.

This is a very easy step to miss, especially when the double negative is somewhat hidden.

What is $7 - (12 - 9)$?

Many people will make the mistake of computing this as $7 - 12 - 9 = -14$. However, notice that the second term in the expression in parentheses has a double negative. Therefore, this expression should be calculated as $7 - 12 + 9 = 4$.

*Manhattan*GMAT Prep
the new standard

> The absolute value of any nonzero number is always positive.

Multiplying & Dividing Signed Numbers

When you multiply or divide two numbers, positive or negative, follow one simple rule:

If **S**igns are the **S**ame, the answer's po**S**itive but if **N**ot, the answer is **N**egative.

$7 \times 8 = 56$ & $(-7) \times (-8) = 56$
$(-7) \times 8 = -56$ & $7 \times (-8) = -56$

$56 \div 7 = 8$ & $-56 \div (-8) = 7$
$56 \div (-7) = -8$ & $-56 \div 8 = -7$

> Remember that when you multiply or divide signed numbers, the NUMBER of negative signs determines the SIGN of the result.

This principle can be extended to multiplication and division by more than two numbers. For example, if 3 numbers are multiplied together, the result will be positive if there are NO negative numbers, or TWO negative numbers. The result will be negative if there are ONE or THREE negative numbers.

We can summarize this pattern as follows. When you multiply or divide a group of nonzero numbers, the result will be positive if you have an EVEN number of negative numbers. The result will be negative if you have an ODD number of negative numbers.

Consider the following Data Sufficiency problem.

> Is the product of all of the elements in Set *S* negative?
>
> (1) All of the elements in Set *S* are negative.
> (2) There are 5 negative numbers in Set *S*.

This is a tricky problem. Based on what we have learned so far, it would seem that Statement (2) tells us that the product must be negative. (5 is an odd number, and when the GMAT says "there are 5" of something, you CAN conclude there are EXACTLY 5 of that thing.) However, if any of the elements in Set *S* equals zero, then the product of the elements in Set *S* will be zero, which is NOT negative. Therefore Statement (2) is INSUFFICIENT.

Statement (1) tells us that all of the numbers in the set are negative. If there are an even number of negatives in Set *S*, the product of its elements will be positive; if there are an odd number of negatives, the product will be negative. This also is INSUFFICIENT.

Combined, we know that Set *S* contains 5 negative numbers and nothing else. SUFFICIENT. The product of the elements in Set *S* must be negative. The correct answer is **(C)**.

Testing Positive & Negative Cases

Some Positives & Negatives problems deal with multiple variables, each of which can be positive or negative. In these situations, you should set up a table listing all the possible positive/negative combinations of the variables, and determine what effect that would have on the question. For example:

> If $ab > 0$, which of the following must be negative?
>
> (A) $a + b$ (B) $|a| + b$ (C) $b - a$ (D) $\dfrac{a}{b}$ (E) $-\dfrac{a}{b}$

One way to solve problems such as this one is to test numbers systematically. In this example, we can test each of the four possible positive/negative combinations of a and b to see whether they meet the criteria established in the question. Then we eliminate any that do not meet these criteria. Finally, we test each of the remaining combinations in each of the answer choices. You can use a chart such as the one below to keep track of your work:

	Criterion: $ab > 0$	**A** $a + b$	**B** $\lvert a \rvert + b$	**C** $b - a$	**D** $\dfrac{a}{b}$	**E** $-\dfrac{a}{b}$
$+, +$ $a = 3$ $b = 6$	YES	POS	POS	POS	POS	(NEG)
$-, +$ $a = -3$ $b = 6$	NO					
$-, -$ $a = -3$ $b = -6$	YES	NEG	NEG	NEG	POS	(NEG)
$+, -$ $a = 3$ $b = -6$	NO					

Use a chart to keep track of positive and negative cases.

Notice that if more than one answer choice gives you the desired result for all cases, you can try another pair of numbers and test those answer choices again.

Another approach to this problem is to determine what you know from the fact that $ab > 0$. If $ab > 0$, then the signs of a and b must both be the same (both positive or both negative).

This should lead you to answer choice (E), since $-\dfrac{a}{b}$ must be negative if a and b have the same sign.

Problem Set

Solve problems #1–5.

1.   Evaluate $2|x - y| + |z + w|$ if $x = 2$, $y = 5$, $z = -3$, and $w = 8$.

2.   Simplify $66 \div (-33) \times |-9|$

3.   Simplify $\dfrac{-30}{5} - \dfrac{18 - 9}{-3}$

4.   Simplify $\dfrac{20 \times (-7)}{-35 \times (-2)}$

5.   When is $|x - 4|$ equal to $4 - x$?

In problems #6–15, decide whether the expression described is POSITIVE, NEGATIVE, or CANNOT BE DETERMINED. If you answer CANNOT BE DETERMINED, give numerical examples to show how the problem could be either positive or negative.

6.   The product of 3 negative numbers

7.   The quotient of one negative and one positive number

8. xy, given that $x < 0$ and $y \neq 0$

9. $|x| \times y^2$, given that $xy \neq 0$

10. $\dfrac{x}{y} \div z$, given that x, y, and z are negative

11. $\dfrac{|ab|}{b}$, given that $b < a < 0$

12. $-4|d|$, given that $d \neq 0$

13. $\dfrac{rst}{w}$, given that $r < s < 0 < w < t$

14. $h^4 k^3 m^2$, given that $k < 0$ and $hm \neq 0$

15. $\dfrac{-x}{(-y)(-z)}$, given that $xyz > 0$

1. **11:** $2|x - y| + |z + w| = 2|2 - 5| + |-3 + 8| = 2|-3| + |5| = 2(3) + 5 = 11$. Note that when you deal with more complicated absolute value expressions, such as $|x - y|$ in this example, you should NEVER change individual signs to "+" signs! For instance, in this problem $|x - y| = |2 - 5|$, not $|2 + 5|$.

2. **−18:** In division, use the Same Sign rule. In this case, the signs are not the same. Therefore, $66 \div (-33)$ yields a negative number (-2). Then, multiply by the absolute value of -9, which is 9. To multiply -2×9, use the Same Sign rule: the signs are not the same, so the answer is negative. Remember to apply division and multiplication from left to right: first the division, then the multiplication.

3. **−3:** This is a two-step subtraction problem. Use the Same Sign rule for both steps. In the first step, the signs are different; therefore, the answer is negative. In the second step, the signs are again different. That result is negative. The final answer is $-6 - (-3) = -3$.

4. **−2:** The sign of the first product, $20 \times (-7)$, is negative (by the Same Sign rule). The sign of the second product, $-35 \times (-2)$, is positive (by the Same Sign rule). Applying the Same Sign rule to the final division problem, the final answer must be negative.

5. $x \leq 4$: Absolute value brackets can only do one of two things to the expression inside of them: (a) leave the expression unchanged, whenever the expression is 0 or positive, or (b) change the sign of the whole expression, whenever the expression is 0 or negative. (Notice that both outcomes occur when the expression is zero, because "negative 0" and "positive 0" are equal.) In this case, the sign of the whole expression $x - 4$ is being changed, resulting in $-(x - 4) = 4 - x$. This will happen only if the expression $x - 4$ is 0 or negative. Therefore $x - 4 \leq 0$, or $x \leq 4$.

6. **NEGATIVE:** The product of the first two negative numbers is positive. A positive times a negative is negative.

7. **NEGATIVE:** By the Same Sign rule, the quotient of a negative and a positive number must be negative.

8. **CANNOT BE DETERMINED:** x is negative. However, y could be either positive or negative. Therefore, we have no way to determine whether the product xy is positive or negative.

9. **POSITIVE:** $|x|$ is positive because absolute value can never be negative, and $x \neq 0$ (since $xy \neq 0$). Also, y^2 is positive because y^2 will be either positive × positive or negative × negative (and $y \neq 0$). The product of two positive numbers is positive, by the Same Sign rule.

10. **NEGATIVE:** Do this problem in two steps: First, a negative number divided by a negative number yields a positive number (by the Same Sign rule). Second, a positive number divided by a negative number yields a negative number (again, by the Same Sign rule).

11. **NEGATIVE:** a and b are both negative. Therefore, this problem is a positive number (by the definition of absolute value) divided by a negative number. By the Same Sign rule, the answer will be negative.

12. **NEGATIVE:** You do not need to know the sign of d to solve this problem. Because d is within the absolute value symbols, you can treat the expression $|d|$ as a positive number (since we know that $d \neq 0$). By the Same Sign rule, a negative number times a positive number yields a negative number.

13. **POSITIVE:** r and s are negative; w and t are positive. Therefore, rst is a positive number. A positive number divided by another positive number yields a positive number.

14. **NEGATIVE:** Nonzero numbers raised to even exponents always yield positive numbers. Therefore, h^4 and m^2 are both positive. Because k is negative, k^3 is negative. Therefore, the final product, $h^4k^3m^2$, is the product of two positives and a negative, which is negative.

15. **NEGATIVE:** Simplifying the original fraction yields: $\dfrac{-x}{yz}$.

If the product xyz is positive, then there are two possible scenarios: (1) all the integers are positive, or (2) two of the integers are negative and the third is positive. Test out both scenarios, using real numbers. In the first case, the end result is negative. In the second case, the two negative integers will essentially cancel each other out. Again, the end result is negative.

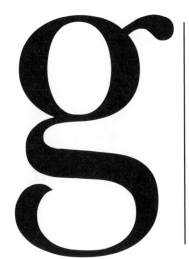

Chapter 4
of
NUMBER PROPERTIES

CONSECUTIVE
INTEGERS

In This Chapter . . .

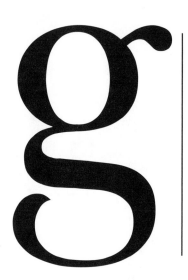

- Evenly Spaced Sets
- Properties of Evenly Spaced Sets
- Counting Integers: Add One Before You Are Done
- The Sum of Consecutive Integers
- Products of Consecutive Integers and Divisibility
- Sums of Consecutive Integers and Divisibility
- Consecutive Integers and Divisibility

CONSECUTIVE INTEGERS

Consecutive integers are integers that follow one after another from a given starting point, without skipping any integers. For example, 4, 5, 6, and 7 are consecutive integers, but 4, 6, 7, and 9 are not. There are many other types of consecutive patterns. For example:

Consecutive Even Integers: 8, 10, 12, 14
(8, 10, 14, and 16 is incorrect, as it skips 12)

Consecutive Primes: 11, 13, 17, 19
(11, 13, 15, and 17 is wrong, as 15 is not prime)

Evenly Spaced Sets

To understand consecutive integers, we should first consider sets of consecutive integers **evenly spaced sets**. These are sequences of numbers whose values go up or down by the same amount (the **increment**) from one item in the sequence to the next. For instance, the set {4, 7, 10, 13, 16} is evenly spaced because each value increases by 3 over the previous value.

Sets of **consecutive multiples** are special cases of evenly spaced sets: all of the values in the set are multiples of the increment. For example, {12, 16, 20, 24} is a set of consecutive multiples because the values increase from one to the next by 4, and each element is a multiple of 4. Note that sets of consecutive multiples must be composed of integers.

Sets of **consecutive integers** are special cases of consecutive multiples: all of the values in the set increase by 1, and all integers are multiples of 1. For example, {12, 13, 14, 15, 16} is a set of consecutive integers because the values increase from one to the next by 1, and each element is an integer.

The relations among evenly spaced sets, consecutive multiples, and consecutive integers are displayed in the diagram to the right:

- All sets of consecutive integers are sets of consecutive multiples.
- All sets of consecutive multiples are evenly spaced sets.
- All evenly spaced sets are fully defined if the following 3 parameters are known:

  (1) The smallest (**first**) or largest (**last**) number in the set

  (2) The **increment** (always 1 for consecutive integers)

  (3) The **number of items** in the set.

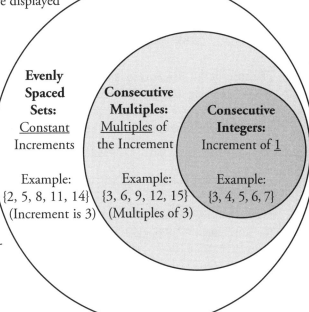

Evenly Spaced Sets: Constant Increments — Example: {2, 5, 8, 11, 14} (Increment is 3)

Consecutive Multiples: Multiples of the Increment — Example: {3, 6, 9, 12, 15} (Multiples of 3)

Consecutive Integers: Increment of 1 — Example: {3, 4, 5, 6, 7}

Consecutive integers and consecutive sets are special types of **evenly spaced sets**. These sets have special properties that are tested on the GMAT.

*ManhattanGMAT*Prep
the new standard

Properties of Evenly Spaced Sets

The following properties apply to **all** evenly spaced sets.

(1) The **arithmetic mean** (average) and **median** are equal to each other. In other words, the average of the elements in the set can be found by figuring out the median, or "middle number."

> What is the arithmetic mean of 4, 8, 12, 16, and 20?

In this example we have 5 consecutive multiples of four. The median is the 3rd largest, or 12. Since this is an evenly spaced set, the arithmetic mean (average) is also 12.

> What is the arithmetic mean of 4, 8, 12, 16, 20, and 24?

In this example we have 6 consecutive multiples of four. The median is the arithmetic mean (average) of the 3rd largest and 4th largest, or the average of 12 and 16. Thus the median is 14. Since this is an evenly spaced set, the average is also 14.

(2) The **mean** and **median** of the set are equal to the **average** of the FIRST and LAST terms.

> What is the arithmetic mean of 4, 8, 12, 16, and 20?

In this example, 20 is the largest (last) number and 4 is the smallest (first). The arithmetic mean and median are therefore equal to $(20 + 4) \div 2 = 12$.

> What is the arithmetic mean of 4, 8, 12, 16, 20, and 24?

In this example, 24 is the largest (last) number and 4 is the smallest (first). The arithmetic mean and median are therefore equal to $(24 + 4) \div 2 = 14$.

Thus for all evenly spaced sets, just remember: the average equals **(First + Last)** $\div$ **2**.

(3) The **sum** of the elements in the set equals the **arithmetic mean** (average) number in the set times the **number of items** in the set.

This property applies to all sets, but it takes on special significance in the case of evenly spaced sets because the "average" is not only the arithmetic mean, but also the median.

> What is the sum of 4, 8, 12, 16, and 20?

We have already calculated the average above; it is equal to 12. There are 5 terms, so the sum equals $12 \times 5 = 60$.

> What is the sum of 4, 8, 12, 16, 20, and 24?

We have already calculated the average above; it is equal to 14. There are 6 terms, so the sum equals $14 \times 6 = 84$.

> *For evenly spaced sets, the median equals the arithmetic mean, and it also equals the average of the first and last numbers in the set.*

ManhattanGMAT Prep
the new standard

Counting Integers: Add One Before You Are Done

How many integers are there from 6 to 10? Four, right? Wrong! There are actually five integers from 6 to 10. Count them and you will see: 6, 7, 8, 9, 10. It is easy to forget that you have to include (or, in GMAT lingo, **be inclusive of**) extremes. In this case, both extremes (the numbers 6 and 10) must be counted. When you merely subtract (10 − 6 = 4), you are forgetting to include the first extreme (6), as it has been subtracted away (along with 5, 4, 3, 2, and 1).

Do you have to methodically count each term in a long consecutive pattern? No. Just remember that if both extremes should be counted, you need to **add one before you are done**.

> How many integers are there from 14 to 765, inclusive?

765 − 14, plus 1, yields 752.

Just remember: for consecutive integers, the formula is **(Last − First + 1)**.

This works easily enough if you are dealing with consecutive integers. Sometimes, however, the question will ask about consecutive multiples. For example, "How many multiples of 4..." or "How many even numbers..." are examples of sets of consecutive multiples.

In this case, if we just subtract the largest number from the smallest and add one, we will be overcounting. For example, "All of the even integers between 12 and 24" yields 12, 14, 16, 18, 20, 22, and 24. That is 7 even integers. However, (Last − First + 1) would yield (24 − 12 + 1) = 13, which is too large. How do we amend this? Since the items in the list are going up by increments of 2 (we are counting only the even numbers), we need to divide (Last − First) by 2. Then, add the one before you are done:

(Last − First) ÷ Increment + 1 = (24 − 12) ÷ 2 + 1 = 6 + 1 = 7.

Just remember: for consecutive multiples, the formula is **(Last − First) ÷ Increment + 1**. The bigger the increment, the smaller the result, because there is a larger gap between the numbers you are counting.

Sometimes, however, it is easier to list the terms of a consecutive pattern and count them, especially if the list is short or if one or both of the extremes are omitted.

> How many multiples of 7 are there between 100 and 150?

Here it may be easiest to list the multiples: 105, 112, 119, 126, 133, 140, 147. Count the number of terms to get the answer: 7. Alternatively, we could note that 105 is the first number, 147 is the last number, and 7 is the increment:

Number of terms = (Last − First) ÷ Increment + 1 = (147 − 105) ÷ 7 + 1 = 6 + 1 = 7.

Memorize the formulas for the number of items in a consecutive set, and also for a set of consecutive integers.

The Sum of Consecutive Integers

Consider this problem:

> What is the sum of all the integers from 20 to 100, inclusive?

Adding all those integers would take much more time than you have for a GMAT problem. Using the rules for evenly spaced sets mentioned before, we can use shortcuts:

(1) Average the first and last term to find the precise "middle" of the set:
$100 + 20 = 120$ and $120 \div 2 = 60$.
(2) Count the number of terms: $100 - 20 = 80$, plus 1 yields 81.
(3) Multiply the "middle" number by the number of terms to find the sum:
$60 \times 81 = 4,860$.

The sum of a set of consecutive integers equals the number of items in the set times the "middle number," or median, of the set.

There are a couple of general facts to note about sums and averages of evenly spaced sets (especially sets of consecutive integers):

- The average of an **odd** number of consecutive integers (1, 2, 3, 4, 5) will always be an integer (3). This is because the "middle number" will be a single integer.
- On the other hand, the average of an **even** number of consecutive integers (1, 2, 3, 4) will never be an integer (2.5), because there is no true "middle number."
- This is because consecutive integers alternate between EVEN and ODD numbers. Therefore, the "middle number" for an even number of consecutive integers is the AVERAGE of two consecutive integers, which is never an integer.

Consider this Data Sufficiency problem:

> Is k^2 odd?
> (1) $k - 1$ is divisible by 2.
> (2) The sum of k consecutive integers is divisible by k.

Statement (1) tells us that $k - 1$ is even. Therefore, k is odd, so k^2 will be odd. SUFFICIENT.

Statement (2) tells us that the sum of k consecutive integers is divisible by k. Therefore, this sum divided by k is an integer. Moreover, the sum of k consecutive integers divided by k is the average (arithmetic mean) of that set of k integers. As a result, Statement (2) is telling us that the average of the k consecutive integers is itself an integer:

$$\frac{(\text{Sum of } k \text{ integers})}{k} = (\text{Average of } k \text{ integers}) = \textbf{Integer}$$

If the average of this set of consecutive integers is an integer, then k must be odd. SUFFICIENT.

The correct answer is **(D)**. EACH statement ALONE is sufficient.

Products of Consecutive Integers and Divisibility

Can you come up with a series of 3 consecutive integers in which none of the integers is a multiple of 3? Go ahead, try it! You will quickly see that any set of 3 consecutive integers must contain one multiple of 3. The result is that the product of any set of 3 consecutive integers is divisible by 3.

$1 \times 2 \times ③ = 6$ $4 \times 5 \times ⑥ = 120$
$2 \times ③ \times 4 = 24$ $5 \times ⑥ \times 7 = 210$
$③ \times 4 \times 5 = 60$ $⑥ \times 7 \times 8 = 336$

According to the Factor Foundation Rule, every number is divisible by all the factors of its factors. If there is always a multiple of 3 in a set of 3 consecutive integers, the product of 3 consecutive integers will always be divisible by 3. Additionally, there will always be at least one multiple of 2 (an even number) in any set of 3 consecutive integers. Therefore, the product of 3 consecutive integers will also be divisible by 2. Thus, the product of 3 consecutive integers will always be divisible by $3! = 3 \times 2 \times 1 = 6$.

The same logic applies to a set of 4 consecutive integers, 5 consecutive integers, and any other number of consecutive integers. For instance, the product of any set of 4 consecutive integers will be divisible by $4! = 4 \times 3 \times 2 \times 1 = 24$, since that set will always contain one multiple of 4, at least one multiple of 3, and another even number (a multiple of 2).

This rule applies to any number of consecutive integers: **The product of *k* consecutive integers is always divisible by *k* factorial (*k*!).**

> The PRODUCT of *n* consecutive integers is divisible by (*n*!). The SUM of *n* consecutive integers is divisible by *n* if *n* is odd, but it is NOT divisible by *n* if *n* is even.

Sums of Consecutive Integers and Divisibility

Find the sum of any 5 consecutive integers:

$4 + 5 + 6 + 7 + 8 = 30$ Notice that both sums are multiples of 5.
$13 + 14 + 15 + 16 + 17 = 75$ In other words, both sums are divisible by 5.

We can generalize this observation. **For any set of consecutive integers with an ODD number of items, the sum of all the integers is ALWAYS a multiple of the number of items.** This is because the sum equals the average times the number of items. For an odd number of integers, the average is an integer, so the sum is a multiple of the number of items. The average of {13, 14, 15, 16, 17} is 15, so $15 \times 5 = 13 + 14 + 15 + 16 + 17$.

Find the sum of any 4 consecutive integers:

$1 + 2 + 3 + 4 = 10$ Notice that NEITHER sum is a multiple of 4.
$8 + 9 + 10 + 11 = 38$ In other words, both sums are NOT divisible by 4.

For any set of consecutive integers with an EVEN number of items, the sum of all the items is NEVER a multiple of the number of items. This is because the sum equals the average times the number of items. For an even number of integers, the average is never an integer, so the sum is never a multiple of the number of items. The average of {8, 9, 10, 11} is 9.5, so $9.5 \times 4 = 8 + 9 + 10 + 11$. That is, $8 + 9 + 10 + 11$ is NOT a multiple of 4.

Consecutive Integers and Divisibility

You can use prime boxes to keep track of factors of consecutive integers. Consider the following problem:

If x is an even integer, is $x(x + 1)(x + 2)$ divisible by 4?

$x(x + 1)(x + 2)$ is the product of 3 consecutive integers, because x is an integer. If there is one even integer in a series of consecutive integers, the product of the series is divisible by 2. If there are two even integers in a series of consecutive integers, the product of the series is divisible by 4. Set up prime boxes:

If x is even then $x + 2$ is even, so 2 is a factor of $x(x + 1)(x + 2)$ twice. Therefore, the product $2 \times 2 = 4$ is a factor of the product of the series. The answer to the question given above is "Yes."

x	$x + 1$	$x + 2$
2		2

Put prime boxes next to each other to show the factors of consecutive integers.

Problem Set

Solve these problems using the rules for consecutive integers.

1.   How many primes are there from 10 to 41, inclusive?

2.   If x, y, and z are consecutive integers, is $x + y + z$ divisible by 3?

3.   What is the sum of all the positive integers up to 100, inclusive?

4.   Will the average of 6 consecutive integers be an integer?

5.   In a sequence of 8 consecutive integers, how much greater is the sum of the last four integers than the sum of the first four integers?

6.   If the sum of a set of 10 consecutive integers is 195, what is the average of the set?

7.   How many terms are there in the set of consecutive integers from -18 to 33, inclusive?

8.   Find the sum of 5 consecutive integers whose average is 50.

9.   If r, s, and t are consecutive positive multiples of 3, is rst divisible by 27, 54, or both?

10.   Is the sum of the integers from 54 to 153, inclusive, divisible by 100?

11.   List at least six factors of the product of 3 consecutive even integers.

12.   If the sum of the last 3 integers in a set of 6 consecutive integers is 624, what is the sum of the first 3 integers of the set?

13.   What is the average of 11 consecutive integers whose sum is -286?

14.   If a, b, c, and d are consecutive integers such that $a < b < c < d$, is $d + a > b + c$?

15.   If the sum of the last 3 integers in a set of 7 consecutive integers is 258, what is the sum of the first 4 integers?

1. **9:** The primes from 10 to 41, inclusive, are: 11, 13, 17, 19, 23, 29, 31, 37, and 41. Note that the primes are NOT evenly spaced, so you have to list them and count them manually.

2. **YES:** For any odd number of consecutive integers, the sum of those integers is divisible by the number of integers. There are 3 consecutive integers (x, y, and z), so the rule applies in this case.

3. **5,050:** There are 100 integers from 1 to 100, inclusive: $(100 - 1) + 1$. (Remember to add one before you are done.) The number exactly in the middle is 50.5. (You can find the middle term by averaging the first and last terms of the set.) Therefore, multiply 100 by 50.5 to find the sum of all the integers in the set: $100 \times 50.5 = 5,050$.

4. **NO:** For any set of consecutive integers with an EVEN number of items, the sum of all the items is NEVER a multiple of the number of items. For example, if we pick 4, 5, 6, 7, 8, and 9:

$$\frac{4 + 5 + 6 + 7 + 8 + 9}{6} = \frac{39}{6} = 6.5$$

5. **16:** Think of the set of 8 consecutive integers as follows: n, $(n + 1)$, $(n + 2)$, $(n + 3)$, $(n + 4)$, $(n + 5)$, $(n + 6)$, and $(n + 7)$.

First, find the sum of the first 4 integers:

$$n + (n + 1) + (n + 2) + (n + 3) = 4n + 6$$

Then, find the sum of the next 4 integers:

$$(n + 4) + (n + 5) + (n + 6) + (n + 7) = 4n + 22$$

The difference between these two partial sums is:

$$(4n + 22) - (4n + 6) = 22 - 6 = 16$$

Another way we could solve this algebraically is to line up the algebraic expressions for each number so that we can subtract one from the other directly:

Sum of the last 4 integers: $(n + 4) + (n + 5) + (n + 6) + (n + 7)$
Less the sum of the first 4 integers: $- [n \quad + (n + 1) + (n + 2) + (n + 3)]$
$$\overline{\quad 4 + \quad\quad 4 + \quad\quad 4 + \quad\quad 4 = 16}$$

Yet another way to see this outcome is to represent the 8 consecutive unknowns with 8 lines:

— — — — ┊ — — — —

Each of the first 4 lines can be matched with one of the second 4 lines, each of which is 4 greater:

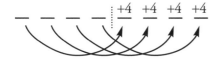

So the sum of the last 4 numbers is $4 \times 4 = 16$ greater that the sum of the first 4.

Finally, you could pick numbers to solve this problem. For example, assume you pick 1, 2, 3, 4, 5, 6, 7, and 8. The sum of the first four numbers is 10. The sum of the last four integers is 26. Again, the difference is $26 - 10 = 16$.

6. **19.5:** Average $= \dfrac{\text{Sum}}{\text{\# of terms}}$. In this problem, we have $\dfrac{195}{10} = 19.5$ as the average.

7. **52:** $33 - (-18) = 51$. Then add one before you are done: $51 + 1 = 52$.

8. **250:** Sum = Average × # of terms: $50 \times 5 = 250$. The fact that the integers are consecutive is not important in this problem.

9. **BOTH:** Because *r*, *s*, and *t* are all multiples of 3, the product *rst* must have THREE 3's as factors. Additionally, at least one of the integers must be even, so the product will have a 2 as a factor, because every other multiple of 3 is even (for example, 3, **6**, 9, **12**, etc.). $27 = 3 \times 3 \times 3$ can be constructed from the known prime factors and is therefore a factor of the product *rst*. $54 = 2 \times 3 \times 3 \times 3$ can also be constructed from the known prime factors and therefore is also factor of the product *rst*.

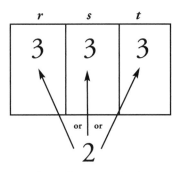

10. **NO:** There are 100 integers from 54 to 153, inclusive. For any even number of consecutive integers, the sum of all the integers is NEVER a multiple of the number of integers. Thus, the sum of the integers 54 to 153 will not be divisible by 100.

11. **(Any six of the following ten factors are acceptable)—1, 2, 3, 4, 6, 8, 12, 16, 24, and 48:**
Because we are dealing with 3 consecutive even numbers, the product must have THREE 2's as prime factors. Additionally, at least one of the numbers MUST be divisible by 4, because we are dealing with consecutive even numbers. Therefore, at least one of the numbers has an additional 2 as a prime factor.

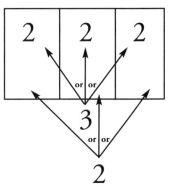

Furthermore, at least one of the integers must be divisible by 3, because there are three consecutive even numbers. Therefore the product will have a 3 as a prime factor.

All told, we know that the product will have at least four 2's and a 3. As we learned in Chapter 1, there are $(4 + 1)(1 + 1) = 10$ different factors of $2^4 \times 3$. Those 10 factors are enumerated in the answer above.

Of course, you could also pick numbers to solve this problem. For example, 2, 4, and 6. The product of these 3 numbers is 48, and any 6 of the 10 factors of 48 will suffice.

12. **615:** Think of the set of integers as *n*, $(n + 1)$, $(n + 2)$, $(n + 3)$, $(n + 4)$, and $(n + 5)$.
$(n + 3) + (n + 4) + (n + 5) = 3n + 12 = 624$. Therefore, $n = 204$.
The sum of the first three integers is: $204 + 205 + 206 = 615$.

Alternatively, another way we could solve this algebraically is to line up the algebraic expressions for each number so that we can subtract one from the other directly:

Sum of the last 3 integers: $\qquad\qquad\qquad\qquad\qquad$ $(n + 3) + (n + 4) + (n + 5)$
Less the sum of the first 3 integers: $\qquad\qquad\qquad$ $- \; [n \qquad + (n + 1) + (n + 2)]$
$$\overline{\qquad\qquad\qquad\qquad\qquad\qquad\quad 3 \; + \quad 3 \; + \quad 3 = 9}$$

Thus the sum of the last 3 numbers is 9 greater than the sum of the first 3 numbers, so the sum of the first 3 numbers is $624 - 9 = 615$.

Visusally, we can represent the 6 consecutive unknowns with 6 lines:

Sum = 624
Average = $624 \div 3 = 208$

205 $\longleftarrow$ 208

Sum = Average $\times$ 3
$= 205 \times 3 = 615$.

13. **−26:** Average $= \dfrac{\text{Sum}}{\text{\# of terms}}$. In this problem, we have $\dfrac{-286}{11} = -26$ as the average.

14. **NO:** Think of the set of integers a, b, c, and d as n, $(n + 1)$, $(n + 2)$, and $(n + 3)$. Substituting these expressions into the inequality, you get: "Is $(n + 3) + n > (n + 1) + (n + 2)$?" This can be simplified: "Is $2n + 3 > 2n + 3$?" These expressions are equal; neither is greater than the other.

15. **330:** Think of the set of integers as n, $(n + 1)$, $(n + 2)$, $(n + 3)$, $(n + 4)$, $(n + 5)$, and $(n + 6)$. $(n + 4) + (n + 5) + (n + 6) = 3n + 15 = 258$. Therefore, $n = 81$. The sum of the first four integers is $81 + 82 + 83 + 84 = 330$.

Alternately: the sum of the first four integers is $4n + 6$. If $n = 81$, then $4n + 6 = 4(81) + 6 = 330$.

g | Chapter 5
of
NUMBER PROPERTIES

EXPONENTS

In This Chapter . . .

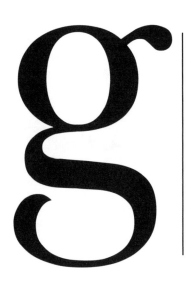

- Wow, That Increased Exponentially!
- All About the Base
- All About the Exponent
- Rules of Exponents
- Simplifying Exponential Expressions
- Common Exponent Errors

EXPONENTS

The mathematical expression 4^3 consists of a base (4) and an exponent (3).

The expression is read as "four to the third power." The base (4) is multiplied by itself as many times as the power requires (3).

Thus $4^3 = 4 \times 4 \times 4 = 64$.

Two exponents have special names: the exponent 2 is called the square, and the exponent 3 is called the cube.

5^2 can be read as five to the second power, or as five squared ($5^2 = 5 \times 5 = 25$).
5^3 can be read as five to the third power, or as five cubed ($5^3 = 5 \times 5 \times 5 = 125$).

Wow, That Increased Exponentially!

Have you ever heard the expression: "Wow, that increased exponentially!"? This phrase captures the essence of exponents. When a positive number greater than 1 increases exponentially, it does not merely increase; it increases a whole lot in a short amount of time.

An important property of exponents is that the greater the exponent, the faster the rate of increase. Consider the following progression:

$5^1 = 5$
$5^2 = 25$ Increased by 20
$5^3 = 125$ Increased by 100
$5^4 = 625$ Increased by 500

The important thing to remember is that, for positive bases bigger than 1, the greater the exponent, the faster the rate of increase.

Just as multiplication is repeated addition, raising a number to a power is simply repeated multiplication.

All About the Base

THE SIGN OF THE BASE
The base of an exponential expression may be either positive or negative. With a negative base, simply multiply the negative number as many times as the exponent requires.

For example:

$$(-4)^2 = (-4) \times (-4) = 16 \qquad\qquad (-4)^3 = (-4) \times (-4) \times (-4) = -64$$

Consider this problem:

If $x^2 = 16$, is x equal to 4?

Your initial inclination is probably to say yes. However, x may not be 4; it may be -4. Thus, we cannot answer the question without additional information. We must be told that x is positive in order to affirm that x is 4. Beware whenever you see an even exponent on the test.

THE EVEN EXPONENT IS DANGEROUS: IT HIDES THE SIGN OF THE BASE!
One of the GMAT's most common tricks involves the even exponent. In many cases, when an integer is raised to a power, the answer keeps the original sign of the base.

Examples:
$3^2 = 9$ $(-3)^3 = -27$ $3^3 = 27$
(positive base,   (negative base,   (positive base,
positive result)   negative result)   positive result)

However, any base raised to an even power will always result in a positive answer. This is because even if the underlying base is negative, there will be an EVEN number of negative signs in the product, and an even number of negative signs in a product makes the product positive.

Examples:
$3^2 = 9$ $(-3)^2 = 9$ $(-3)^4 = 81$
(positive base,   (negative base,   (negative base,
positive result)   positive result)   positive result)

Therefore, when a base is raised to an even exponent, the resulting answer may either keep or change the original sign of the base. Whether $x = 3$ or -3, $x^2 = 9$. This makes even exponents extremely dangerous, and the GMAT loves to try to trick you with them.

Note that odd exponents are harmless, since they always keep the original sign of the base. For example, if you have the equation $x^3 = 64$, you can be sure that $x = 4$. You know that x is not -4 because $(-4)^3$ would yield -64.

A BASE OF 0, 1, or −1
- An exponential expression with a base of 0 always yields 0, regardless of the exponent.
- An exponential expression with a base of 1 always yields 1, regardless of the exponent.
- An exponential expression with a base of −1 yields 1 when the exponent is even, and yields −1 when the exponent is odd.

For example, $0^3 = 0 \times 0 \times 0 = 0$ and $0^4 = 0 \times 0 \times 0 \times 0 = 0$.
Similarly, $1^3 = 1 \times 1 \times 1 = 1$ and $1^4 = 1 \times 1 \times 1 \times 1 = 1$.
Finally, $(-1)^3 = (-1) \times (-1) \times (-1) = -1$, but $(-1)^4 = (-1) \times (-1) \times (-1) \times (-1) = 1$.

Thus, if you are told that $x^6 = x^7 = x^{15}$, you know that x must be either 0 or 1. Do not try to do algebra on the equation. Simply plug 0 and 1 to check that the equation makes sense. Note that −1 does not fit the equation, since $(-1)^6 = 1$, but $(-1)^7 = -1$.

Of course, if you are told that $x^6 = x^8 = x^{10}$, x could be 0, 1 *or* −1. Any one of these three values fits the equation as given. (See why even exponents are so dangerous?)

A FRACTIONAL BASE
When the base of an exponential expression is a positive proper fraction (in other words, a fraction between 0 and 1), an interesting thing occurs: as the exponent increases, the value of the expression decreases!

$$\left(\frac{3}{4}\right)^1 = \frac{3}{4} \qquad\qquad \left(\frac{3}{4}\right)^2 = \frac{3}{4} \times \frac{3}{4} = \frac{9}{16} \qquad\qquad \left(\frac{3}{4}\right)^3 = \frac{3}{4} \times \frac{3}{4} \times \frac{3}{4} = \frac{27}{64}$$

Notice that $\frac{3}{4} > \frac{9}{16} > \frac{27}{64}$. Increasing powers cause positive fractions to decrease.

We could also distribute the exponent before multiplying. For example:

$$\left(\frac{3}{4}\right)^1 = \frac{3^1}{4^1} = \frac{3}{4} \qquad\qquad \left(\frac{3}{4}\right)^2 = \frac{3^2}{4^2} = \frac{9}{16} \qquad\qquad \left(\frac{3}{4}\right)^3 = \frac{3^3}{4^3} = \frac{27}{64}$$

Note that, just like proper fractions, decimals between 0 and 1 decrease as their exponent increases:

$$(0.6)^2 = 0.36 \qquad\qquad (0.5)^4 = 0.0625 \qquad\qquad (0.1)^5 = 0.00001$$

A COMPOUND BASE
When the base of an exponential expression is a product, we can multiply the base together and then raise it to the exponent, OR we can distribute the exponent to each number in the base.

$$\left(2 \times 5\right)^3 = (10)^3 = 1,000 \qquad\textbf{OR}\qquad \left(2 \times 5\right)^3 = 2^3 \times 5^3 = 8 \times 125 = 1,000$$

You cannot do this with a sum, however. You must add the numbers inside the parentheses first.

$$\left(2 + 5\right)^3 = (7)^3 = 343 \qquad\qquad \left(2 + 5\right)^3 \neq 2^3 + 5^3 \text{ !!!}$$

While most positive numbers increase when raised to higher exponents, numbers between 0 and 1 decrease.

All About the Exponent

ADDING EXPONENTS

When we multiply terms with the same base, we add the exponents. For example:

$$3^4 \times 3^2 = 3^{(4+2)} = 3^6$$
$$3^4 \times 3^2 = (3 \times 3 \times 3 \times 3) \times (3 \times 3) = 3^6$$

Rule: When multiplying two terms with the same base, combine exponents by adding.

SUBTRACTING EXPONENTS

When we divide terms with the same base, we subtract the exponents. For example:

$$3^6 \div 3^2 = 3^{(6-2)} = 3^4$$
$$3^6 \div 3^2 = (3 \times 3 \times 3 \times 3 \times 3 \times 3) \div (3 \times 3) = 3^4$$

Rule: When dividing two terms with the same base, combine exponents by subtracting.

NESTED EXPONENTS

A base raised to "nested" exponents means that the base is raised to one exponent, usually inside parentheses, and then that value is raised to another exponent.

For example: $\left(3^2\right)^4$

When we apply two exponents in a row to one base, we multiply the exponents.

$$
\begin{aligned}
\left(3^2\right)^4 &= (3^2)(3^2)(3^2)(3^2) \\
&= (3 \times 3)(3 \times 3)(3 \times 3)(3 \times 3) \\
&= 3 \times 3 \times 3 \times 3 \times 3 \times 3 \times 3 \times 3 = 3^8 \\
&= (3)^{2 \times 4}
\end{aligned}
$$

Rule: When raising a power to a power, combine exponents by multiplying.

THE SIGN OF THE EXPONENT

An exponent is not always positive. What happens if the exponent is negative?

$$5^{-1} = \frac{1}{5^1} = \frac{1}{5} \qquad \frac{1}{4^{-2}} = \frac{1}{\frac{1}{4^2}} = 4^2 = 16 \qquad (-2)^{-3} = \frac{1}{(-2)^3} = -\frac{1}{8}$$

Very simply, negative exponents mean "put the term containing the exponent in the denominator of a fraction, and make the exponent positive." In other words, we divide by the base a certain number of times, rather than multiply. An expression with a negative exponent is the reciprocal of what that expression would be with a positive exponent. **When you see a negative exponent, think reciprocal!**

$$\left(\frac{3}{4}\right)^{-3} = \left(\frac{4}{3}\right)^3 = \frac{64}{27}$$

Raising a number to a negative exponent is the same as raising the number's reciprocal to the equivalent positive exponent.

AN EXPONENT OF 1
Any base raised to the exponent of 1 keeps the original base. This is fairly intuitive.

$$3^1 = 3 \qquad 4^1 = 4 \qquad (-6)^1 = -6 \qquad \left(-\frac{1}{2}\right)^1 = -\frac{1}{2}$$

However, a fact that is not always obvious is that **any number that does not have an exponent implicitly has an exponent of 1**.

$$3 \times 3^4 = ?$$

In this case, just pretend that the "3" term has an exponent of 1 and proceed as before.

$$3^1 \times 3^4 = 3^{(1+4)} = 3^5 \qquad \text{Likewise, } 3 \times 3^x = 3^1 \times 3^x = 3^{(1+x)} = 3^{x+1}$$

Rule: When you see a base without an exponent, write in an exponent of 1.

AN EXPONENT OF 0
By definition, any nonzero base raised to the 0 power yields 1. This may not seem intuitive.

$$3^0 = 1 \qquad 4^0 = 1 \qquad (-6)^0 = 1 \qquad \left(-\frac{1}{2}\right)^0 = 1$$

To understand this fact, think of division of a number by itself, which is one way a zero exponent could occur.

$$\frac{3^7}{3^7} = 3^{(7-7)} = 3^0 = 1$$

When we divide 3^7 by itself, the result equals 1. Also, by applying the subtraction rule of exponents, we see that 3^7 divided by itself yields 3^0. Therefore, 3^0 MUST equal 1.

Note also that 0^0 is indeterminate and **never** appears on the GMAT. Zero is the ONLY number that, when raised to the zero power, does not necessarily equal 1.

Rule: Any nonzero base raised to the power of zero (e.g. 3^0) is equal to 1.

FRACTIONAL EXPONENTS
Fractional exponents are the link between exponents and roots, which are discussed in the next chapter. Within the exponent fraction, the **numerator** tells us what **power** to raise the base to, and the **denominator** tells us which **root** to take. You can raise the base to the power and take the root in EITHER order.

What is $25^{3/2}$?

The numerator of the fraction is 3, so we should raise 25 to the 3rd power. The denominator is 2, so we need to take the square root of 25^3. Note that we can rewrite 25^3 as $(5^2)^3$:

$$25^{3/2} = \sqrt{25^3} = \sqrt{(5^2)^3} = 5^3 = 125. \text{ We can also write } 25^{3/2} = \left(5^2\right)^{3/2} = 5^{2 \times \frac{3}{2}} = 5^3 = 125.$$

> Fractional exponents are the link between exponents and roots: the numerator tells what power to raise the base to, and the denominator tells what root to take.

Rules of Exponents

There are many ways to combine exponents, as we have already seen. For each rule, you should memorize both the **algebraic rule** and **an example expression** that you can imitate to simplify more complicated expressions.

Many of the numerical examples look very different from the algebraic rules from which they are derived. For instance, knowing that $x^n \cdot y^n = (xy)^n$ may not help you recognize that $2^4 \cdot 3^4 = 6^4$. In fact, it could be easy to make a mistake by combining the expression incorrectly:

> **INCORRECT:** $2^4 \cdot 3^4 = 6^{(4+4)} = 6^8$
> **INCORRECT:** $2^4 \cdot 3^4 = (2+3)^{(4+4)} = 5^8$

Again, $2^4 \cdot 3^4 = (2 \times 3)^4 = 6^4$ is correct.

Follow the examples to simplify harder problems. For instance, let us say you need to factor 10^3 into primes. Doing so with the rule $x^n \cdot y^n = (xy)^n$ can be intimidating, but following the numerical example $2^4 \cdot 3^4 = 6^4$ would allow you to conclude easily that $10^3 = 5^3 \cdot 2^3$. (In this case, we are applying the exponent rule in reverse. We are breaking the expression down into factors, while in the numerical example, we are combining them. You need to be able to go in either direction when manipulating exponential expressions.)

Exponent Rule	Examples
$x^a \cdot x^b = x^{a+b}$	$c^3 \cdot c^5 = c^8 \qquad 3^5 \cdot 3^8 = 3^{13}$ $5(5^n) = 5^1(5^n) = 5^{n+1}$
$a^x \cdot b^x = (ab)^x$	$2^4 \cdot 3^4 = 6^4 \qquad 12^5 = 2^{10} \cdot 3^5$
$\dfrac{x^a}{x^b} = x^{(a-b)}$	$\dfrac{2^5}{2^{11}} = \dfrac{1}{2^6} = 2^{-6} \qquad \dfrac{x^{10}}{x^3} = x^7$
$\left(\dfrac{a}{b}\right)^x = \dfrac{a^x}{b^x}$	$\left(\dfrac{10}{2}\right)^6 = \dfrac{10^6}{2^6} = 5^6 \qquad \dfrac{3^5}{9^5} = \left(\dfrac{3}{9}\right)^5 = \left(\dfrac{1}{3}\right)^5$
$(a^x)^y = a^{xy} = (a^y)^x$	$(3^2)^4 = 3^{2\cdot 4} = 3^8 = 3^{4\cdot 2} = (3^4)^2$
$x^{-a} = \dfrac{1}{x^a}$	$\left(\dfrac{3}{2}\right)^{-2} = \left(\dfrac{2}{3}\right)^2 = \dfrac{4}{9} \qquad 2x^{-4} = \dfrac{2}{x^4}$
$x^{a/b} = \sqrt[b]{x^a} = \left(\sqrt[b]{x}\right)^a$	$27^{4/3} = \sqrt[3]{27^4} = \left(\sqrt[3]{27}\right)^4 = 3^4 = 81$ $\sqrt[5]{x^{15}} = x^{15/5} = x^3$
$a^x + a^x + a^x = 3a^x$	$3^4 + 3^4 + 3^4 = 3 \cdot 3^4 = 3^5$ $3^x + 3^x + 3^x = 3 \cdot 3^x = 3^{x+1}$

This last property applies in other situations. For example, $2^3 + 2^3 = 2(2^3) = 2^4$, and $4^x + 4^x + 4^x + 4^x = 4(4^x) = 4^{x+1}$.

*Manhattan*GMAT*Prep*
the new standard

Simplifying Exponential Expressions

Now that you have the basics down for working with bases and exponents, what about working with multiple exponential expressions at the same time? If two (or more) exponential terms in an expression have a base in common or an exponent in common, you can often simplify the expression. (In this section, by "simplify," we mean "reduce to one term.")

WHEN CAN YOU SIMPLIFY EXPONENTIAL EXPRESSIONS?

(1)   You can only **simplify** exponential expressions that are linked by multiplication or division. You cannot **simplify** expressions linked by addition or subtraction (although in some cases, you can **factor** them and otherwise manipulate them).

(2)   You can simplify exponential expressions linked by multiplication or division if they have either a base or an exponent in common.

HOW CAN YOU SIMPLIFY THEM?

Use the exponent rules described earlier. If you forget these rules, you can derive them on the test by writing out the example exponential expressions.

Same bases or exponents can be simplified if the terms are MULTIPLIED or DIVIDED. Otherwise, look for ways to factor the terms.

These expressions CANNOT be simplified:	**These expressions CAN be simplified:**
$7^4 + 7^6$	$(7^4)(7^6)$
$3^4 + 12^4$	$(3^4)(12^4)$
$6^5 - 6^3$	$\dfrac{6^5}{6^3}$
$12^7 - 3^7$	$\dfrac{12^7}{3^7}$

Use the rules outlined above to simplify the expressions in the right column:

$$(7^4)(7^6) = 7^{4+6} = 7^{10}$$

$$(3^4)(12^4) = (3 \times 12)^4 = 36^4$$

$$\frac{6^5}{6^3} = 6^{5-3} = 6^2$$

$$\frac{12^7}{3^7} = \frac{(3 \times 2 \times 2)^7}{3^7} = 3^{7-7}(2 \times 2)^7 = 3^0 4^7 = 4^7$$

We can simplify all the expressions in the right-hand column to a single term, because the terms are multiplied or divided. The expressions in the left-hand column **cannot be simplified**, because the terms are added or subtracted. However, they **can be factored** whenever the base is the same. For example, $7^4 + 7^6$ can be factored because the two terms in the expression have a factor in common. What factor exactly do they have in common? Both terms contain 7^4. If we factor 7^4 out of each term, we are left with $7^4(7^2 + 1) = 7^4(50)$.

The terms can ALSO be factored whenever the exponent is the same and the terms contain something in common in the base. For example, $3^4 + 12^4$ can be factored because $12^4 = (2 \times 2 \times 3)^4$. Thus both bases contain 3^4, and the factored expression is $3^4(1 + 4^4)$.

Likewise, $6^5 - 6^3$ can be factored as $6^3(6^2 - 1)$ and $12^7 - 3^7$ can be factored as $3^7(4^7 - 1)$.

On the GMAT, it generally pays to factor exponential terms that have something in common in the bases.

> If $x = 4^{20} + 4^{21} + 4^{22}$, what is the largest prime factor of x?

All three terms contain 4^{20}, so we can factor the expression: $x = 4^{20}(4^0 + 4^1 + 4^2)$. Therefore, $x = 4^{20}(1 + 4 + 16) = 4^{20}(21) = 4^{20}(3 \times 7)$. The largest prime factor of x is 7.

Common Exponent Errors

Study this list of common errors carefully and identify any mistakes that you occasionally make. Note the numerical examples given!

INCORRECT	CORRECT
$(x + y)^2 = x^2 + y^2$? $(3 + 2)^2 = 3^2 + 2^2 = 13$?	$(x + y)^2 = x^2 + 2xy + y^2$ $(3 + 2)^2 = 3^2 + 2(3)(2) + 2^2 = 25$
$a^x \cdot b^y = (ab)^{x+y}$? $2^4 \cdot 3^5 = (2 \cdot 3)^{4+5}$?	Cannot be simplified further (different bases **and** different exponents)
$a^x \cdot a^y = a^{xy}$? $5^4 \cdot 5^3 = 5^{12}$?	$a^x \cdot a^y = a^{x+y}$ $5^4 \cdot 5^3 = 5^7$
$(a^x)^y = a^{(x+y)}$? $(7^4)^3 = 7^7$?	$(a^x)^y = a^{xy}$ $(7^4)^3 = 7^{12}$
$a^x + a^y = a^{x+y}$? $x^3 + x^2 = x^5$?	Cannot be simplified further (addition **and** different exponents)
$a^x + a^x = a^{2x}$? $2^x + 2^x = 2^{2x}$?	$a^x + a^x = 2a^x$ $2^x + 2^x = 2(2^x) = 2^{x+1}$
$a \cdot a^x = a^{2x}$? $5 \cdot 5^z = 25^z$?	$a \cdot a^x = a^{x+1}$ $5 \cdot 5^z = 5^{z+1}$
$-x^2 = x^2$? $-4^2 = 16$?	$-x^2$ cannot be simplified further $-4^2 = -16$ **Compare:** $(-x)^2 = x^2$ **and** $(-4)^2 = 16$
$a \cdot b^x = (a \cdot b)^x$? $2 \cdot 3^4 = (2 \cdot 3)^4$?	Cannot be simplified further

Problem Set

Simplify or otherwise reduce the following expressions using the rules of exponents.

1. 2^{-5}

2. $8^{5/3}$

3. $9^{-1/2}$

4. $\left(\dfrac{4}{9}\right)^{-3/2}$

5. $\dfrac{7^6}{7^4}$

6. $8^4(5^4)$

7. $2^4 \times 2^5 \div 2^7 - 2^4$

8. $\dfrac{9^4}{3^4} + \left(4^2\right)^3$

Solve the following problems.

9. Does $a^2 + a^4 = a^6$ for all values of a?

10. $x^3 < x^2$. Describe the possible values of x.

11. If $x^4 = 16$, what is $|x|$?

12. If $y^5 > 0$, is $y < 0$?

13. If $b > a > 0$, and $c \neq 0$, is $a^2 b^3 c^4$ positive?

14. Simplify: $\dfrac{y^2 \times y^5}{(y^2)^4}$

15. If $r^3 + |r| = 0$, what are the possible values of r?

1. **1/32:** Remember that a negative exponent yields the reciprocal of the same expression with a positive exponent. $2^{-5} = \dfrac{1}{2^5} = \dfrac{1}{32}$

2. **32:** $8^{5/3} = \sqrt[3]{8^5} = \left(\sqrt[3]{8}\right)^5 = 2^5 = 32$

3. $\dfrac{1}{3}$: $\; 9^{-\frac{1}{2}} = \dfrac{1}{9^{\frac{1}{2}}} = \dfrac{1}{\sqrt{9}} = \dfrac{1}{3}$

4. $\dfrac{27}{8}$: $\; \left(\dfrac{4}{9}\right)^{-\frac{3}{2}} = \left(\dfrac{9}{4}\right)^{\frac{3}{2}} = \sqrt{\left(\dfrac{9}{4}\right)^3} = \left(\sqrt{\dfrac{9}{4}}\right)^3 = \left(\dfrac{3}{2}\right)^3 = \dfrac{3^3}{2^3} = \dfrac{27}{8}$

5. **49:** $\dfrac{7^6}{7^4} = 7^{6-4} = 7^2 = 49$

6. **2,560,000:** $8^4(5^4) = 40^4 = 2,560,000$

7. **−12:** $\dfrac{2^4 \times 2^5}{2^7} - 2^4 = 2^{(4+5-7)} - 2^4 = 2^2 - 2^4 = 2^2(1 - 2^2) = 4(1 - 4) = -12.$

8. **4,177:** $\dfrac{9^4}{3^4} + \left(4^2\right)^3 = 3^4 + 4^6 = 81 + 4,096 = 4,177$

9. **NO:** Remember, you cannot combine exponential expressions linked by addition.

10. **Any non-zero number less than 1:** As positive proper fractions are multiplied, their value decreases. For example, $(1/2)^3 < (1/2)^2$. Also, any negative number will make this inequality true. A negative number cubed is negative. Any negative number squared is positive. For example, $(-3)^3 < (-3)^2$. The number zero itself, however, does not work, since $0^3 = 0^2$.

11. **2:** The possible values for x are 2 and −2. The absolute value of both 2 and −2 is 2.

12. **NO:** An integer raised to an odd exponent retains the original sign of the base. Therefore, if y^5 is positive, y is positive.

13. **YES:** b and a are both positive numbers. Whether c is positive or negative, c^4 is positive. (Recall that any number raised to an even power is positive.) Therefore, the product $a^2 b^3 c^4$ is the product of 3 positive numbers, which will be positive.

14. $\dfrac{1}{y}$: $\; \dfrac{y^2 \times y^5}{(y^2)^4} = \dfrac{y^7}{y^8} = y^{7-8} = y^{-1} = \dfrac{1}{y}$

15. **0,−1:** If $r^3 + |r| = 0$, then r^3 must be the opposite of $|r|$. The only values for which this would be true are 0, which is the opposite of itself, and −1, whose opposite is 1.

g

Chapter 6
of
NUMBER PROPERTIES

ROOTS

In This Chapter . . .

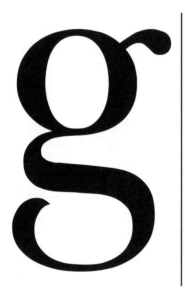

- A Square Root Has Only One Value
- Roots and Fractional Exponents
- Simplifying a Root
- Imperfect vs. Perfect Squares
- Simplifying Roots of Imperfect Squares
- Estimating Roots of Imperfect Squares
- Properties of Roots
- Common Root Errors
- Memorize: Squares and Square Roots
- Memorize: Cubes and Cube Roots

ROOTS

A root (also called a radical) is the opposite of an exponent, in a sense.

$\sqrt[3]{64}$ is an expression that answers the question: What number, when multiplied by itself three times, will yield 64?

The answer is 4, because $4 \times 4 \times 4 = 64$. Thus $\sqrt[3]{64} = 4$. We can say that 4 is the cube root of 64.

The most common type of root is a square root: $\sqrt{64}$. Notice that a square root is so common that it is written without the small 2 on the outside of the radical symbol. The expression $\sqrt{64}$ means: What number, when multiplied by itself, will yield 64? The answer is 8, because $8 \times 8 = 64$. Thus, the square root of 64 is 8.

Since square roots have only one solution, they are less tricky and dangerous than even exponents.

A Square Root Has Only One Value

Unlike even exponents, which yield both a positive and a negative solution, roots have only one solution. For example:

If $\sqrt{4} = x$, what is x?

In the above example, $x = 2$, since $(2)(2) = 4$. While it is true that $(-2)(-2) = 4$, the GMAT follows the standard convention of mathematics. When we take an **even root** (a square root, a 4th root, a 6th root, etc.), a radical sign means ONLY the nonnegative root of a number. Thus, the number 2 is the only solution for x. -2 is NOT a solution for this problem. When you see a square root symbol on the GMAT, think only the positive root. (In contrast, when you decide to unsquare an equation with even exponents, you must consider both positive and negative solutions. For instance, the equation $x^2 = 4$ has two solutions: $x = 2$ and $x = -2$.)

For **odd roots** (cube root, 5th root, 7th root, etc.), the root will have the same sign as the base.

If $\sqrt[3]{-27} = x$, what is x?

The correct answer is -3, because $(-3)(-3)(-3) = -27$.

Note that there is no solution for the even root of a negative number. No number, when multiplied an even number of times, can possibly be negative.

Rule: Even roots only have a positive value. $\sqrt{4} = 2$, NOT ± 2.

A root can only have a negative value if (1) it is an odd root and (2) the base of the root is negative. For example, $\sqrt[3]{-27} = -3$.

Roots and Fractional Exponents

As we discussed in the previous chapter, fractional exponents are the link between roots and exponents. Within the exponent fraction, the **numerator** tells us what **power** to raise the base to, and the **denominator** tells us which **root** to take. You can raise the base to the power and take the root in EITHER order.

> What is $216^{1/3}$?

The numerator of the fraction is 1, so we should not raise the base to any power. The denominator is 3, so we need to take the 3rd (cube) root of 216^1. In order to determine that root, we should break 216 into prime factors:

$$216 = 3 \times 3 \times 3 \times 2 \times 2 \times 2 = 6^3.$$

The 3rd root of 216 is 6, so $216^{1/3} = \sqrt[3]{216} = 6$.

> What is $\left(\dfrac{1}{8}\right)^{-4/3}$?

Because the exponent is negative, we must take the reciprocal of the base of $\left(\dfrac{1}{8}\right)$ and change the exponent to its positive equivalent. Then we must take the 3rd (cube) root to the 4th power:

$$\left(\frac{1}{8}\right)^{-4/3} = 8^{4/3} = \sqrt[3]{8^4} = \left(\sqrt[3]{8}\right)^4 = 2^4 = 16$$

You should know how to express fractional exponents in terms of roots and powers, but you should also know how to express roots as fractional exponents. The resulting expression may be much easier to simplify. Just remember that a root becomes the denominator of a fractional exponent.

> Express $\sqrt[4]{\sqrt{x}}$ as a fractional exponent.

To transform the expression into fractional exponents, you should transform the individual roots into exponents. The square root is equivalent to an exponent of 1/2, and the fourth root is equivalent to an exponent of 1/4. Therefore, this expression becomes $\left(x^{1/2}\right)^{1/4}$, or $x^{1/8}$. Note that this is equivalent to $\sqrt[8]{x}$.

*Manhattan*GMAT*Prep
the new standard

Simplifying a Root

Sometimes there are two numbers inside the radical sign. In order to simplify this type of root, it is often helpful to split up the numbers into two roots and then solve. At other times, the opposite is true: you have two roots that you would like to simplify by combining them under one radical sign.

WHEN CAN YOU SIMPLIFY ROOTS?

You can only simplify roots by combining or separating them in multiplication and division. You cannot combine or separate roots in addition or subtraction.

HOW CAN YOU SIMPLIFY THEM?

When multiplying roots, you can split up a larger product into its separate factors. Creating two separate radicals and simplifying each one individually before multiplying can save you from having to compute large numbers. Similarly, you can also simplify two roots that are being multiplied together into a single root of the product. For example:

$$\sqrt{25 \times 16} = \sqrt{25} \times \sqrt{16} = 5 \times 4 = 20$$

$$\sqrt{50} \times \sqrt{18} = \sqrt{50 \times 18} = \sqrt{900} = 30$$

Notice in the second example that by combining the roots first, we found a perfect square under the radical. Thus, we could simply take the square root of that number, rather than having to deal with multiple radicals in an intermediate step towards the solution.

Division of roots works the same way. You can split a larger quotient into the dividend and divisor. You can also combine two roots that are being divided into a single root of the quotient. For example:

$$\sqrt{144 \div 16} = \sqrt{144} \div \sqrt{16} = 12 \div 4 = 3$$

$$\sqrt{72} \div \sqrt{8} = \sqrt{72 \div 8} = \sqrt{9} = 3$$

The GMAT may try to trick you into splitting the sum or difference of two numbers inside a radical into two individual roots. Also, the GMAT may try to trick you into combining the sum or difference of two roots inside one radical sign. **Remember that you may only separate or combine the <u>product</u> or <u>quotient</u> of two roots. You cannot separate or combine the <u>sum</u> or <u>difference</u> of two roots.** For example:

INCORRECT: $\sqrt{16 + 9} = \sqrt{16} + \sqrt{9} = 4 + 3 = 7 ?$

CORRECT: $\sqrt{16 + 9} = \sqrt{25} = 5$

Imperfect vs. Perfect Squares

Not all square roots yield an integer. For example: $\sqrt{52}$ does not yield an integer answer because no integer multiplied by itself will yield 52. The number 52 is an example of an imperfect square, because its square root is not an integer.

> Multiple roots can be combined whenever the roots are multiplied or divided.

Simplifying Roots of Imperfect Squares

Some imperfect squares can be simplified into multiples of smaller square roots. For an imperfect square such as $\sqrt{52}$, we can rewrite $\sqrt{52}$ as a product of primes under the radical.

$$\sqrt{52} = \sqrt{2 \times 2 \times 13}$$

We can simplify any pairs inside the radical. In this case, there is a pair of 2's. Since $\sqrt{2 \times 2} = \sqrt{4} = 2$, we can rewrite $\sqrt{52}$ as follows:

$$\sqrt{52} = \sqrt{2 \times 2 \times 13} = 2 \times \sqrt{13}$$

This is often written as $2\sqrt{13}$. Let us look at another example:

Simplify $\sqrt{72}$.

We can rewrite $\sqrt{72}$ as a product of primes: $\sqrt{72} = \sqrt{2 \times 2 \times 2 \times 3 \times 3}$. Since there are a pair of 2's and a pair of 3's inside the radical, we can simplify them. We are left with: $\sqrt{72} = 2 \times 3 \times \sqrt{2} = 6\sqrt{2}$.

It is usually better to simplify roots than to estimate them, unless the question asks for an estimated numerical value.

Estimating Roots of Imperfect Squares

If you have to estimate the root of an imperfect square, there are a couple of considerations to make. First, if you have a simple square root—that is, a square root without a coefficient in front—then you can estimate it by figuring out the two closest perfect squares on either side of it. For example:

Estimate $\sqrt{52}$.

The first step is to find the closest perfect squares square roots that you **do** know. We know that $\sqrt{49} = 7$ and $\sqrt{64} = 8$. Thus we can estimate that $\sqrt{52}$ is between 7 and 8. A good estimate might be 7.1 or 7.2. (Notice that we estimated the number to be closer to 7 than to 8, because $\sqrt{52}$ is closer to $\sqrt{49}$ than it is to $\sqrt{64}$.)

If you want to estimate a square root that is multiplied by a coefficient, then you could simply estimate the square root itself (as above) and then multiply that estimate by the coefficient. However, you can often get a more accurate estimate by combining the coefficient with the root.

Estimate $4\sqrt{5}$.

Using the fact that $\sqrt{5}$ is between 2 and 3, and then multiplying by 4, yields an estimate between 8 and 12—a large margin of error. Instead, combine the root and the coefficient:

$$4\sqrt{5} = \sqrt{16} \times \sqrt{5} = \sqrt{80}$$

Because $\sqrt{80}$ is slightly less than $\sqrt{81}$, we know that $\sqrt{80}$ is slightly less than 9, or about 8.9.

Properties of Roots

Several properties of roots govern how roots can be manipulated and simplified. For each rule, you should memorize both the **algebraic rule** and **an example expression** that you can imitate to simplify more complicated expressions.

Property of Roots	Numerical Examples
$\dfrac{\sqrt[n]{x}}{\sqrt[n]{y}} = \sqrt[n]{\dfrac{x}{y}}$	$\dfrac{\sqrt{10}}{\sqrt{5}} = \sqrt{\dfrac{10}{5}} = \sqrt{2}$ $\dfrac{\sqrt[3]{16}}{\sqrt[3]{2}} = \sqrt[3]{\dfrac{16}{2}} = \sqrt[3]{8} = 2$
$\sqrt[n]{x} \cdot \sqrt[n]{y} = \sqrt[n]{xy}$	$\sqrt{10} \cdot \sqrt{5} = \sqrt{50}$ $\sqrt[3]{24} \cdot \sqrt[3]{9} = \sqrt[3]{216} = 6$
$\sqrt[b]{x^a} = \left(\sqrt[b]{x}\right)^a = x^{a/b}$	$25^{3/2} = \sqrt{25^3} = 5^3 = 125$ $49^{-1/2} = \dfrac{1}{\sqrt{49}} = \dfrac{1}{7}$ $\sqrt[5]{x^{15}} = x^{15/5} = x^3$

MEMORIZE the rules and errors of manipulating roots—also memorize the examples!

Common Root Errors

Separate errors involving the manipulation of roots are commonly made. You should study these errors carefully and determine whether you occasionally make these errors. Otherwise, you may find yourself trying to performing illegal manipulations on roots.

INCORRECT	CORRECT
$\sqrt{x+y} = \sqrt{x} + \sqrt{y}$? $\sqrt{4+9} = \sqrt{4} + \sqrt{9} = 2 + 3 = 5$?	$\sqrt{x+y}$ cannot be simplified. $\sqrt{4+9} = \sqrt{13}$
$\sqrt{x-y} = \sqrt{x} - \sqrt{y}$? $\sqrt{25-4} = \sqrt{25} - \sqrt{4} = 5 - 2 = 3$?	$\sqrt{x-y}$ cannot be simplified. $\sqrt{25-4} = \sqrt{21}$
$\sqrt[b]{x^a} = x^{a-b}$? $\sqrt[5]{2^{20}} = 2^{20-5} = 2^{15}$?	$\sqrt[b]{x^a} = x^{a/b}$ $\sqrt[5]{2^{20}} = 2^{20/5} = 2^4$

Memorize: Squares and Square Roots

You should memorize the following squares and square roots, as they often appear on the GMAT.

$1^2 = 1$	$\sqrt{1} = 1$
$1.4^2 \approx 2$	$\sqrt{2} \approx 1.4$
$1.7^2 \approx 3$	$\sqrt{3} \approx 1.7$
$2.25^2 \approx 5$	$\sqrt{5} \approx 2.25$
$2^2 = 4$	$\sqrt{4} = 2$
$3^2 = 9$	$\sqrt{9} = 3$
$4^2 = 16$	$\sqrt{16} = 4$
$5^2 = 25$	$\sqrt{25} = 5$
$6^2 = 36$	$\sqrt{36} = 6$
$7^2 = 49$	$\sqrt{49} = 7$
$8^2 = 64$	$\sqrt{64} = 8$
$9^2 = 81$	$\sqrt{81} = 9$
$10^2 = 100$	$\sqrt{100} = 10$
$11^2 = 121$	$\sqrt{121} = 11$
$12^2 = 144$	$\sqrt{144} = 12$
$13^2 = 169$	$\sqrt{169} = 13$
$14^2 = 196$	$\sqrt{196} = 14$
$15^2 = 225$	$\sqrt{225} = 15$
$16^2 = 256$	$\sqrt{256} = 16$
$20^2 = 400$	$\sqrt{400} = 20$
$25^2 = 625$	$\sqrt{625} = 25$
$30^2 = 900$	$\sqrt{900} = 30$

Memorize: Cubes and Cube Roots

You should memorize the following cubes and cube roots, as they often appear on the GMAT.

$1^3 = 1$	$\sqrt[3]{1} = 1$
$2^3 = 8$	$\sqrt[3]{8} = 2$
$3^3 = 27$	$\sqrt[3]{27} = 3$
$4^3 = 64$	$\sqrt[3]{64} = 4$
$5^3 = 125$	$\sqrt[3]{125} = 5$

Problem Set

1. For each of these statements, indicate whether the statement is TRUE or FALSE:

   (a) If $x^2 = 11$, then $x = \sqrt{11}$.

   (b) If $x^3 = 11$, then $x = \sqrt[3]{11}$.

   (c) If $x^4 = 16$, then $x = 2$.

   (d) If $x^5 = 32$, then $x = 2$.

Solve or simplify the following problems, using the properties of roots.

2. $\sqrt[3]{8}$

3. $\sqrt{18} \div \sqrt{2}$

4. $\sqrt{75}$

5. $27^{4/3}$

6. $\left(\dfrac{1}{81}\right)^{-1/4}$

7. $\sqrt{63} + \sqrt{28}$

8. $\sqrt{20} \times \sqrt{5}$

9. $\sqrt[3]{100 - 36}$

10. Estimate $\sqrt{60}$ to the nearest tenth.

11. $\sqrt{20a} \times \sqrt{5a}$, assuming a is positive.

12. $10\sqrt{12} \div 2\sqrt{3}$

13. $\sqrt[3]{-1}$

14. $\sqrt{x^2y^3 + 3x^2y^3}$, assuming x and y are positive.

15. $\sqrt{0.0081}$

1. (a) **FALSE:** Even exponents hide the sign of the original number, because they always result in a positive value. If $x^2 = 11$, then $|x| = \sqrt{11}$. Thus x could be either $\sqrt{11}$ or $-\sqrt{11}$.

(b) **TRUE:** Odd exponents preserve the sign of the original expression. Therefore, if x^3 is positive, then x must itself be positive. If $x^3 = 11$, then x must be $\sqrt[3]{11}$.

(c) **FALSE:** Even exponents hide the sign of the original number, because they always result in a positive value. If $x^4 = 16$, then x could be either 2 or −2.

(d) **TRUE:** Odd exponents preserve the sign of the original expression. Therefore, if x^5 is positive, then x must itself be positive. If $x^5 = 32$, then x must be 2.

2. **2:** The cube root of 8 is the number that, when multiplied by itself three times, yields 8.

3. **3:** $\sqrt{18} \div \sqrt{2} = \sqrt{9} = 3$

4. **$5\sqrt{3}$:** $\sqrt{75} = \sqrt{25} \times \sqrt{3} = 5\sqrt{3}$

5. **81:** $27^{4/3} = \sqrt[3]{27^4} = \left(\sqrt[3]{27}\right)^4 = 3^4 = 81$

6. **3:** $\left(\dfrac{1}{81}\right)^{-1/4} = 81^{1/4} = \sqrt[4]{81} = 3$

7. **$5\sqrt{7}$:** $\sqrt{63} + \sqrt{28} = (\sqrt{9} \times \sqrt{7}) + (\sqrt{4} \times \sqrt{7}) = 3\sqrt{7} + 2\sqrt{7} = 5\sqrt{7}$

8. **10:** $\sqrt{20} \times \sqrt{5} = \sqrt{20 \times 5} = \sqrt{100} = 10$

9. **4:** $\sqrt[3]{100 - 36} = \sqrt[3]{64} = 4$

10. **7.8:** 60 is in between two perfect squares: 49, which is 7^2, and 64, which is 8^2. Note that 60 is quite close to 8^2. Therefore, a reasonable estimate for $\sqrt{60}$ is 7.8.

11. **$10a$:** $\sqrt{20a} \times \sqrt{5a} = \sqrt{100a^2} = 10a$

12. **10:** $10\sqrt{12} \div 2\sqrt{3} = \dfrac{10(\sqrt{4} \times \sqrt{3})}{2\sqrt{3}} = \dfrac{20\sqrt{3}}{2\sqrt{3}} = 10$

13. **−1:** Since $(-1)(-1)(-1) = -1$, the cube root of −1 is −1. (Cube roots can be negative numbers.)

14. **$2xy\sqrt{y}$:** Notice that we have two terms under the radical that both contain x^2y^3. We can add like terms together if they are under the same radical: $\sqrt{y^3 + 3x^2y^3} = \sqrt{(1+3)x^2y^3} = \sqrt{4x^2y^3}$. Now, factor out all squares and isolate them under their own radical sign: $\sqrt{4x^2y^3} = \sqrt{4} \times \sqrt{x^2} \times \sqrt{y^2} \times \sqrt{y} = 2xy\sqrt{y}$. (Note that since x and y are positive, $\sqrt{x^2} = x$ and $\sqrt{y^2} = y$.)

15. **0.09:** Since $(0.09)(0.09) = 0.0081$, $\sqrt{0.0081} = 0.09$. You can also rewrite 0.0081 as 81×10^{-4}:

$$\sqrt{81 \times 10^{-4}} = \sqrt{81} \times \sqrt{10^{-4}} = 9 \times \left(10^{-4}\right)^{1/2} = 9 \times 10^{-2} = 0.09$$

g | Chapter 7
of
NUMBER PROPERTIES

PEMDAS

In This Chapter . . .

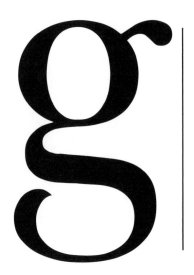

- PEMDAS: Order of Operations

- Subtraction of Expressions

- Fraction Bars as Grouping Symbols

A Note About PEMDAS: Order of Operations

On the GMAT, you need to know the correct order of operations when simplifying an expression. The correct order of operations is: Parentheses-Exponents-(Multiplication-Division)-(Addition-Subtraction). Multiplication and division are in parentheses because they are on the SAME level of priority. The same is true of addition and subtraction.

$$\text{Simplify } 5 + (2 \times 4 + 2)^2 - |7(-4)| + 18 \div 3 \times 5 - 8.$$

P = PARENTHESES. First, perform all the operations that are INSIDE parentheses. Note that in terms of order of operations, **absolute value signs are equivalent to parentheses**. In this expression, there are two groups of parentheses:

$(2 \times 4 + 2)$ and $|7(-4)|$

In the first group, there are two operations to perform, multiplication and addition. Using PEMDAS, we see that multiplication must come before addition.

$(2 \times 4 + 2) = (8 + 2) = 10$

In the second group, there is only one operation: multiplication. We do this and then we find the absolute value.

$|7(-4)| = |-28| = 28$

Now our original expression looks like this:

$5 + 10^2 - 28 + 18 \div 3 \times 5 - 8$

E = EXPONENTS. Second, take care of any exponents in the expression. Our expression only has one exponent.

$10^2 = 100$

Now our expression looks like this:

$5 + 100 - 28 + 18 \div 3 \times 5 - 8$

M&D = MULTIPLICATION & DIVISION. Next, we perform all the multiplication and division. It is important to note that multiplication does NOT necessarily come before division. **A group of multiplication and division operations must be performed from left to right**. The division symbol ($\div$) is rare on the GMAT, but you should be familiar with it nonetheless.

$18 \div 3 \times 5$
$\underbrace{\qquad}$
$6 \quad \times 5 = 30$

Now our expression reads:

$5 + 100 - 28 + 30 - 8$

A&S = ADDITION & SUBTRACTION. Lastly, we perform all the addition and subtraction. It is important to note here again that addition does NOT necessarily come before subtraction. **A group of addition and subtraction operations must be performed from left to right**.

$5 + 100 - 28 + 30 - 8$
$105 - 28 + 30 - 8$
$77 + 30 - 8$
$107 - 8$

After performing PEMDAS, we arrive at our answer:

99

An easy way to remember this order is by the word PEMDAS. Or you can think of the phrase "Please Excuse My Dear Aunt Sally."

*Manhattan*GMAT*Prep
the new standard

Subtraction of Expressions

One of the most common errors involving orders of operations occurs when an expression with multiple terms is subtracted. The subtraction must occur across EVERY term within the expression. Each term in the subtracted part must have its sign reversed. For example:

$x - (y - z) = x - y + z$ (note that the signs of both y and $-z$ have been reversed)
$x - (y + z) = x - y - z$ (note that the signs of both y and z have been reversed)
$x - 2(y - 3z) = x - 2y + 6z$ (note that the signs of both y and $-3z$ have been reversed)

What is $5x - [y - (3x - 4y)]$?

Both expressions in parentheses must be subtracted, so the signs of each term must be reversed for EACH subtraction. Note that the square brackets are just fancy parentheses, used so that we avoid having parentheses right next to each other.

$$5x - [y - (3x - 4y)] =$$
$$5x - (y - 3x + 4y) =$$
$$5x - y + 3x - 4y = \mathbf{8x - 5y}$$

Be sure to distribute the subtraction all the way through each term in a subtracted expression.

Fraction Bars as Grouping Symbols

Even though fraction bars do not fit into the PEMDAS hierarchy, they do take precedence. In any expression with a fraction bar, you should **pretend that there are parentheses around the numerator and denominator of the fraction**. This may be obvious as long as the fraction bar remains in the expression, but it is easy to forget if you eliminate the fraction bar or add or subtract fractions.

Simplify: $\dfrac{x-1}{2} - \dfrac{2x-1}{3}$

The common denominator for the two fractions is 6, so multiply the numerator and denominator of the first fraction by 3, and those of the second fraction by 2:

$$\frac{x-1}{2}\left(\frac{3}{3}\right) - \frac{2x-1}{3}\left(\frac{2}{2}\right) = \frac{3x-3}{6} - \frac{4x-2}{6}$$

Treat the expressions $3x - 3$ and $4x - 2$ as though they were enclosed in parentheses! Accordingly, once you make the common denominator, actually put in parentheses for these numerators. Then reverse the signs of both terms in the second numerator:

$$\frac{(3x-3)-(4x-2)}{6} = \frac{3x-3-4x+2}{6} = \frac{-x-1}{6} = -\frac{x+1}{6}$$

Problem Set

1. Evaluate $-3x^2$, $-3x^3$, $3x^2$, $(-3x)^2$, and $(-3x)^3$ if $x = 2$, and also if $x = -2$.

2. Evaluate $(4 + 12 \div 3 - 18) - [-11 - (-4)]$.

3. Which of the parentheses in the following expressions are unnecessary and could thus be removed without any change in the value of the expression?

    (a) $-(5^2) - (12 - 7)$
    (b) $(x + y) - (w + z) - (a \times b)$

4. Evaluate $-|-13 - (-17)|$.

5   Evaluate $\left[\dfrac{4+8}{2-(-6)}\right] - [4 + 8 \div 2 - (-6)]$.

6. Simplify: $x - (3 - x)$.

7. Simplify: $(4 - y) - 2(2y - 3)$.

8. Solve for x: $2(2 - 3x) - (4 + x) = 7$.

9. Solve for x: $x\left(x - \dfrac{5x+6}{x}\right) = 0$.

10. Solve for z: $\dfrac{4z-7}{3-2z} = -5$.

1.

If $x = 2$:	If $x = -2$:
$-3x^2 = -3(4) = \mathbf{-12}$	$-3x^2 = -3(4) = \mathbf{-12}$
$-3x^3 = -3(8) = \mathbf{-24}$	$-3x^3 = -3(-8) = \mathbf{24}$
$3x^2 = 3(4) = \mathbf{12}$	$3x^2 = 3(4) = \mathbf{12}$
$(-3x)^2 = (-6)^2 = \mathbf{36}$	$(-3x)^2 = 6^2 = \mathbf{36}$
$(-3x)^3 = (-6)^3 = \mathbf{-216}$	$(-3x)^3 = 6^3 = \mathbf{216}$

Remember that exponents are evaluated before multiplication! Watch not only the order of operations, but also the signs in these problems.

2. **−3:** $(4 + 12 \div 3 - 18) - [-11 - (-4)] =$

$(4 + 4 - 18) - (-11 + 4) =$ division before addition/subtraction

$(-10) - (-7) =$ subtraction of negative = addition

$-10 + 7 = \mathbf{-3}$ arithmetic—watch the signs!

3. **(a):** The parentheses around 5^2 are unnecessary, because this exponential is performed before the negation (which counts as multiplying by –1) and before the subtraction. The other parentheses are necessary, because they cause the right-hand subtraction to be performed before the left-hand subtraction. Without them, the two subtractions would be performed from left to right.

(b): The first and last pairs of parentheses are unnecessary. The addition is performed before the neighboring subtraction by default, because addition and subtraction are performed from left to right. The multiplication is the first operation to be performed, so the right-hand parentheses are completely unnecessary. The middle parentheses are necessary to ensure that the addition is performed before the subtraction that comes to the left of it.

4. **−4:** $-|13 - (-17)| =$

$-|13 + 17| =$

$-|4| = \mathbf{-4}$ subtraction of negative = addition

     arithmetic

Note that the absolute value CANNOT be made into 13 + 17. You must perform the arithmetic inside grouping symbols FIRST, whether inside parentheses or inside absolute-value bars. THEN you can remove the grouping symbols.

*Manhattan*GMAT*Prep
the new standard

5. $-\dfrac{25}{2}:$

$$-\dfrac{25}{2}: \left[\dfrac{4+8}{2-(-6)}\right]-\left[4+8\div2-(-6)\right]=$$

$$\left(\dfrac{4+8}{2+6}\right)-\left(4+8\div2+6\right)=$$ subtraction of negative = addition

$$\left(\dfrac{12}{8}\right)-\left(\dfrac{4+4+6}{}\right)=$$ fraction bar acts as a grouping symbol

$$\dfrac{3}{2}-14=$$ arithmetic

$$\dfrac{3}{2}-\dfrac{28}{2}=-\dfrac{25}{2}$$ arithmetic

6. **$2x-3$:** Do not forget to reverse the signs of every term in a subtracted expression.

$$x-(3-x)=x-3+x=2x-3$$

7. **$-5y+10$ (or $10-5y$):** Do not forget to reverse the signs of every term in a subtracted expression.

$$(4-y)-2(2y-3)=4-y-4y+6=-5y+10 \text{ (or } 10-5y)$$

8. **-1:** $\quad 2(2-3x)-(4+x)=7 \qquad\qquad -7x=7$

$\qquad\qquad 4-6x-4-x=7 \qquad\qquad\qquad x=-1$

9. **$x=\{6,-1\}$:** Distribute the multiplication by x. Note that, when you cancel the x in the denominator, the quantity $5x+6$ is implicitly enclosed in parentheses!

$$x\left(x-\dfrac{5x+6}{x}\right)=0 \qquad\qquad (x-6)(x+1)=0$$

$$x^2-(5x+6)=0 \qquad\qquad\qquad x=\textbf{6 or }-1$$

$$x^2-5x-6=0$$

Note also that the value 0 is impossible for x, because x is in a denominator by itself in the original equation. We are not allowed to divide by 0. Do not look at the product in the original equation and deduce that $x=0$ is a solution.

10. **4/3:**

$$\dfrac{4z-7}{3-2z}=-5$$

$$4z-7=-5(3-2z)$$

$$4z-7=-15+10z$$

$$8=6z$$

$$z=8/6=4/3$$

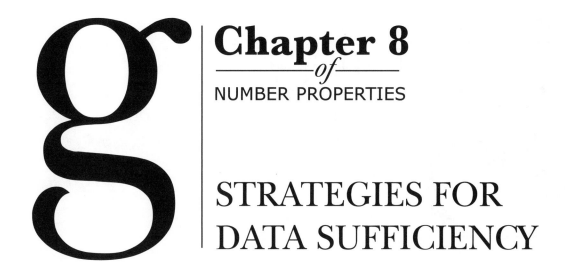

Chapter 8
of
NUMBER PROPERTIES

STRATEGIES FOR
DATA SUFFICIENCY

In This Chapter . . .

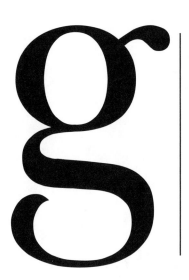

Rephrasing

Data sufficiency problems involve an element of disguise, in which the mathematical content and information are obscured in some way. Therefore, your first task in solving a data sufficiency problem is to rephrase the question and/or the statements whenever possible.

In problems that deal with number properties, you can often rephrase the question to incorporate familiar rules, such as the ones you have studied in this strategy guide. For example:

> If p is an integer, is $\dfrac{p}{18}$ an integer?
>
> (1) $\dfrac{5p}{18}$ is an integer.
>
> (2) $\dfrac{6p}{18}$ is an integer.

Rephrase both the question AND the statements, if you can.

(A) Statement (1) ALONE is sufficient, but statement (2) alone is not sufficient.
(B) Statement (2) ALONE is sufficient, but statement (1) alone is not sufficient.
(C) BOTH statements TOGETHER are sufficient, but NEITHER statement ALONE is sufficient.
(D) EACH statement ALONE is sufficient.
(E) Statements (1) and (2) together are NOT sufficient.

If $\dfrac{p}{18}$ is an integer, this means that p is DIVISIBLE by 18. Thus, this question is asking whether p is divisible by 18.

The prime factorization of 18 is $3 \times 3 \times 2$. In order for the integer p to be divisible by 18, it must be divisible by two 3's and a 2. Using the prime box strategy explained earlier in this guide, we can rephrase the question as follows:

Are there two 3's and a 2 in the prime box of p?

Now, we can rephrase each statement.

Statement (1) can be restated as $5p$ is divisible by 18, or by two 3's and a 2. A double prime box, as shown to the right, allows you to separate the factors of a larger product.

The coefficient of 5 does not provide ANY of the necessary primes to be divisible by 18 (in other words, it does not have any 3's or 2's as factors). Therefore, in order for $5p$ to be divisible by 18, p must be divisible by two 3's and a 2. Thus, statement (1) can be rephrased:

There are (at least) two 3's and a 2 in the prime box of p.

This is sufficient to answer the question.

Statement (2) can be restated as *6p* is divisible by 18 or by two 3's and a 2. A double prime box, as shown to the right, allows you to separate the factors of a larger product.

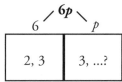

The coefficient of 6 provides two of the necessary primes to be divisible by 18 (6 has a factor of 3 and a factor of 2). Therefore, in order for *6p* to be divisible by 18, *p* must be divisible by one 3. While there may be additional primes in the prime box of p, statement (2) only *guarantees* one 3 in *p*'s prime box. Thus, statement (2) can be rephrased:

There is (at least) one 3 in the prime box of *p*.

This is not sufficient to answer the question. Thus, the answer to this data sufficiency problem is (A): Statement (1) ALONE is sufficient, but statement (2) alone is not sufficient.

Another way to solve this problem is to test numbers (discussed later in this section): think of the smallest possible value of *p* that fits each statement. For Statement (1), the smallest value of *p* such that $\frac{5p}{18}$ is an integer is 18. The next number for which $\frac{5p}{18}$ is an integer is 36. Therefore, it seems that *p* needs to be a multiple of 18 to fit the criteria of the statement, so the statement is sufficient. However, for Statement (2), *p* could equal 18, but it could also equal 3. In either case, $\frac{6p}{18}$ is an integer. Therefore, *p* does not have to be a multiple of 18, so Statement (2) is not sufficient. Again, the correct answer is (A): Statement (1) ALONE is sufficient.

The preceding problem tests your knowledge of divisibility. However, the mathematical content being tested is disguised. Rephrasing allows you to remove that disguise and to demonstrate your knowledge of number properties. Let us look at another example:

> If *x* is a positive integer, is $x^3 - 3x^2 + 2x$ divisible by 4?
>
> > (1) $x = 4y + 4$, where *y* is an integer
> > (2) $x = 2z + 2$, where *z* is an integer

Rephrase the question by factoring:

$$x^3 - 3x^2 + 2x = x(x^2 - 3x + 2) = x(x - 1)(x - 2)$$

This series represents three consecutive integers: *x* − 2, *x* − 1, and *x*. Therefore, the question is really asking:

Is the product of three consecutive integers, *x* − 2, *x* − 1, and *x*, divisible by 4?

*Manhattan*GMAT*Prep
the new standard

One way that the product of 3 consecutive integers will be divisible by 4 is if 2 of those integers are even. For this to be the case in the product above, the first and last of the consecutive integers ($x - 2$ and x) must be even.

Thus, an even better rephrasing may be this:

Is x even?

Note: It is possible that x is not even and the product is still divisible by 4. This would be the case if the middle integer, $x - 1$, is a multiple of 4. We might incorporate this possibility separately by adding a second part to our rephrased question as follows:

Is x even?   OR   Is $x - 1$ a multiple of 4?

However, the GMAT rarely requires you to consider such complicated, multi-part questions with non-overlapping scenarios. You might think that the GMAT would love to write such questions, testing one possibility with Statement (1) and the other possibility with Statement (2). However, the statements **cannot contradict** each other. In other words, you cannot have something like these two statements:

(1) x is even.
(2) $x - 1$ is a multiple of 4.

Thus, you typically only have to worry about the simpler question.

Now let us rephrase the statements.

Statement (1) tells us that $x = 4y + 4$, where y is an integer.

Since y is an integer, $4y$ must be a multiple of 4. Adding another 4 to a multiple of 4 means that the result will also be a multiple of 4. Thus, x is a multiple of 4, which means that x is even.

Statement (1) can be rephrased as follows: **x is even.** This is sufficient to answer our rephrased question.

Statement (2) tells us that $x = 2z + 2$, where z is an integer.

Since z is an integer, $2z$ must be a multiple of 2. Adding another 2 to a multiple of 2 means that the result will also be a multiple of 2. Thus, x is a multiple of 2, which means that x is even.

Statement (2) can be rephrased as follows: **x is even.** This is sufficient to answer our rephrased question.

Therefore, the answer to this data sufficiency problem is (D): EACH statement ALONE is sufficient. The second possibility (that $x - 1$ might be a multiple of 4) was never tested. This outcome is typical.

To rephrase a statement, take the given information, reduce it into its simplest form, and focus on how the piece of information relates to the question.

Types of Data Sufficiency Problems: Value vs. Yes/No

There are two types of data sufficiency problems:

(1) VALUE: These questions require you to solve for one numerical value:

What is the value of $x + y$?
How old is Vera?
In what year were the most rabbits born?

The information in the statements can be considered sufficient if it allows you to find a single number to answer the question. If the information yields more than one value, the information is insufficient.

(2) YES/NO: These questions require you to give a simple yes or no answer:

Is n divisible by 17?
Is $x + y$ prime?
Is $y < 0$?

In a Yes/No data sufficiency problem, YES is a sufficient answer and NO is a sufficient answer. MAYBE is not a sufficient answer.

The information in the statements can be considered sufficient if it allows you to conclusively answer YES or NO. If the answer is MAYBE, the information is insufficient.

As you rephrase Data Sufficiency questions, **never turn a Yes/No question into a Value question**. The reason is that you can answer many Yes/No questions about a number without knowing exactly what the value of the number is. For example, if we know that x is greater than 10, we can answer the question, "Is x positive?" without knowing exactly what the value of x is.

Testing Numbers

Another strategy that is helpful for solving data sufficiency problems that deal with number properties is to test numbers. As you test numbers, try to prove that the statements are NOT SUFFICIENT. That is, try to find examples that yield multiple answers to a VALUE question or that make the answer to a YES/NO question MAYBE. If you can do this, you can conclude that the statement or statements are NOT SUFFICIENT. Here is an example:

If n is an integer and n^3 is between 1 and 100, inclusive, what is the value of n?

(1) $n = 2k + 1$, where k is an integer.
(2) n is a prime number.

In this problem, we are working with a small list of possibilities: integers whose cubes are between 1 and 100. The only integers that meet this criteria are 1, 2, 3, and 4, as shown in the box to the right. The simplest way to solve this problem is to use the information given in each statement to test this list. If the information eliminates all but one value, it is sufficient; if it yields multiple values, it is not sufficient.

$$1^3 = 1$$
$$2^3 = 8$$
$$3^3 = 27$$
$$4^3 = 64$$

Statement (1) tells us that *n* can be any odd number. The general expression for an even integer is $2k$, where k is any integer; the general expression for an odd integer is $2k + 1$. Therefore, of the four values on the list, *n* could be 1 or 3. Since statement (1) yields two possible values, it is NOT sufficient to answer the question.

Statement (2) tells us that *n* is a prime number, so *n* could be either 2 or 3. Statement (2) yields two possible values, so it is NOT sufficient either.

If we look at both statements together, *n* must be equal to 3, the intersection of the two statements. Statement (1) eliminates the possibility that *n* is 2 or 4. Statement (2) eliminates the possibility that *n* is 1 or 4. We are left with only one value: *n* must be equal to 3.

The answer to this data sufficiency problem is (C): BOTH statements TOGETHER are sufficient, but NEITHER statement ALONE is sufficient.

Test Smart Numbers

When testing numbers, you should be trying to prove the statement insufficient. So, be sure to try fractions, negatives, and zero, unless you are **specifically** told in the question that the variables have constraints: they represent only integers, only positive numbers, only nonzero numbers, etc.

When you are using a number-testing strategy, try your best to find numbers that yield multiple answers for a Value question, or a MAYBE answer for a YES/NO question. If you can do so, you have proven the statement insufficient. If you cannot do so, and you have picked numbers wisely, it is likely that the statement is sufficient. If you have exhausted ALL possibilities in your search, you can be more certain that the statement is sufficient.

Is $x^2 \leq 2x$?

(1) $x > 0$
(2) $x < 3$

Without diving into algebra theory, we can think through this problem by picking numbers. For example, Statement (1) says that $x > 0$. By picking $x = 1$ and $x = 5$, we can see that Statement (1) is not sufficient because we get different answers to the question (1^2 is less than 2×1, but 5^2 is greater than 2×5). INSUFFICIENT.

Similarly, for Statement (2), we can pick numbers to prove insufficiency. Let us pick $x = 1$ and $x = -3$ (remember, *x* does not have to be positive because we are not explicitly told in the question that *x* must be positive). We can see that 1^2 is less than 2×1, but $(-3)^2$ is greater than $2 \times (-3)$. INSUFFICIENT.

Combining the statements, *x* must be between 0 and 3. Is this sufficient? The only integers that fit both statements are $x = 1$ and $x = 2$. In both cases, x^2 is less than or equal to $2x$. HOWEVER, **there is no restriction in this problem demanding that x be an integer**. Therefore, we need to test non-integers as well. If we pick $x = 2.5$, for example, we get $x^2 = 6.25$ and $2x = 5$. Thus, x^2 will be greater than $2x$ if *x* is a non-integer between 2 and 3. INSUFFICIENT. The correct answer is (E): Statements (1) and (2) TOGETHER are NOT sufficient.

The Statements Never Contradict Each Other

A final strategy is to use the fact that the two statements in a data sufficiency problem will never contradict each other, as previously noted.

If y and n are positive integers, is yn divisible by 7?

> (1) $n^2 - 14n + 49 = 0$
> (2) $n + 2$ is the first of three consecutive integers whose product is 990.

The two data sufficiency statements always provide TRUE information; therefore, the two statements cannot contradict each other.

Statement (1) can be factored: $n^2 - 14n + 49 = (n - 7)(n - 7) = 0$, so $n = 7$. Since $n = 7$ and y is an integer, yn must be divisible by 7. Statement (1) is sufficient to answer the question: YES, yn is divisible by 7.

Statement (2) tells us that the product of $(n + 2)$, $(n + 3)$, and $(n + 4)$ is equal to 990. If we test numbers, we find that the three consecutive integers whose product is 990 are 9, 10, and 11. (The fact that 990 is close to 1000 should provide a hint that the three numbers should be close to 10, which is $\sqrt[3]{1,000}$.)

Now let us say that we *incorrectly* identify n as 9, the first of the three consecutive integers. If $n = 9$, then we do not know whether yn is divisible by 7. MAYBE it is (if y is divisible by 7) or MAYBE it is not (if y is not divisible by 7). We conclude that statement (2) is not sufficient to answer the question.

Thus, we would identify the answer to this data sufficiency question as (A): Statement (1) ALONE is sufficient, but statement (2) alone is not sufficient.

But wait! Take a look again at the information we derived from each statement. Statement (1) told us that $n = 7$, while statement (2) told us that $n = 9$. This is not possible because the two data sufficiency statements on the GMAT always provide TRUE information. The two statements cannot contradict each other.

Whenever you find that your two statements contradict each other, it means that you have made a mistake! What mistake did we make in the logic above?

Our mistake here was in statement (2). We forgot that $n + 2$ (not n) is the first of the three consecutive integers. Thus, $n + 2 = 9$, which means that $n = 7$. Now statement (2) no longer contradicts statement (1). Knowing that $n = 7$ means that yn must be divisible by 7. Thus, statement (2) IS in fact sufficient to answer the question.

Using the principle that the two data sufficiency statements cannot contradict each other, we caught our mistake. The correct answer is actually (D): EACH statement ALONE is sufficient.

Rephrasing: Challenge Short Set

In Chapter 9 and Chapter 13, you will find lists of NUMBER PROPERTIES problems that have appeared on past official GMAT exams. These lists refer to problems from three books published by the Graduate Management Admission Council® (the organization that develops the official GMAT exam):

The Official Guide for GMAT Review, 12th Edition
The Official Guide for GMAT Quantitative Review
The Official Guide for GMAT Quantitative Review, 2nd Edition
<u>Note</u>: The two editions of the Quant Review book largely overlap. Use one OR the other. The questions contained in these three books are the property of The Graduate Management Admission Council, which is not affiliated in any way with Manhattan GMAT.

As you work through the Data Sufficiency problems in these lists, be sure to focus on *rephrasing*. If possible, try to *rephrase* each question into its simplest form *before* looking at the two statements. In order to rephrase, focus on figuring out the specific information that is absolutely necessary to answer the question. After rephrasing the question, you should also try to *rephrase* each of the two statements, if possible. Rephrase each statement by simplifying the given information into its most basic form.

In order to help you practice rephrasing, we have taken a set of generally difficult Data Sufficiency problems on *The Official Guide* problem list (these are the problem numbers listed in the "Challenge Short Set" on page 177) and have provided you with our own sample rephrasings for each question and statement. In order to evaluate how effectively you are using the rephrasing strategy, you can compare your rephrased questions and statements to our own rephrasings that appear below. Questions and statements that are significantly rephrased appear in **bold**.

You should attempt to do the Official Guide problems **prior** to reading our sample rephrasings. Also note that for many questions, the rephrasing that you come up with may differ slightly from what is written in this text. That does not necessarily mean that your rephrasing is incorrect; some questions can be rephrased in multiple ways. But be sure to note any problems in which your rephrasing led to an incorrect answer.

Rephrasings from *The Official Guide For GMAT Review, 12th Edition*

The questions and statements that appear below are only our *rephrasings*. The original questions and statements can be found by referencing the problem numbers below in the Data Sufficiency section of *The Official Guide for GMAT Review, 12th Edition* (pages 272–288).

76. **Is any of the variables m, p, or t even?**

     (1) $t + m = $ even
   Either t and m are both even, or they are both odd.

     (2) $t - m = $ even
   Either t and m are both even, or they are both odd.

82. **Is 5 a factor of either x or y?**

     (1) **3 is a factor of x.**

     (2) **5 is a factor of y.**

90. Do t and 12 share any prime factors?
   Is 2 or 3 a factor of t?

     (1) $t = 2k + 3m = 2 \times 3 \times$ integer $+ 3m = 3x (2x \times$ integer $+ 3)$
   t is a multiple of 3

     (2) $t = 2k + 3m = 2k + 3 \times 3 \times$ integer
   t could be a multiple of 2 or 3

106. **Is either x or y even?**

     (1) x and y are consecutive integers.
   One of the variables is even, and the other is odd.

     (2) $x = y \times$ even
   $x = $ even

128. **Is n divisible by m?**

     (1) **$3n$ is divisible by m**

     (2) **$13n$ is divisible by m**

166.　Is $\dfrac{1}{10^n} < \dfrac{1}{100}$?

Is $\dfrac{1}{10^n} < \dfrac{1}{10^2}$?

Is $n > 2$?

(1) $n > 2$

(2) $(1/10)^n \times (1/10)^{-1} < 1/10$
　　　$(1/10)^n \times 10 < 1/10$
　　　　$(1/10)^n < 1/100$
　　　　　$1/10^n < 1/10^2$
　　　　　　$n > 2$

170.　Is the product of consecutive integers $(n + 1)n(n - 1)$ divisible by 4?
　　OR: Are there 2 even integers in the set of consecutive integers $(n + 1)$, n, $(n - 1)$?
　　OR: (Best) **Is n odd?**

(1) n is an even number plus 1
　　n is odd

(2) $n(n + 1)$ is divisible by 6.
　　Either n OR $n + 1$ is even.

171.　What is the tens digit of positive integer x?
　　No meaningful rephrasing can be done to the question.

(1) **$x = 100m + 30$ where m is a nonnegative integer**

(2) **$x = 110n + 30$ where n is a nonnegative integer**

172.　**Are x and y different (one even and one odd)?**

(1) **x and z are the same (either both even or both odd)**

(2) **y and z are different (one even and one odd)**

Rephrasings from *The Official Guide for GMAT Quantitative Review, 2nd Edition*

The questions and statements that appear below are only our *rephrasings*. The original questions and statements can be found by referencing the problem numbers below in the Data Sufficiency section of *The Official Guide for GMAT Quantitative Review, 2nd Edition* (pages 152–163). First Edition numbers are included in parentheses. Problems unique to one edition are so indicated.

3.   **How many factors does *n* have?**
(3.)

    (1)

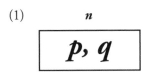

n has only 2 factors other than 1 and *n*: *p* and *q*.
Since *p* and *q* are prime, there are no other factors.
Thus, ***n* has 4 factors**.

    (2) *n* has the same number of factors as 8; thus, ***n* has 4 factors**.

31.   **Is *x* a perfect square?**
(116.)

    (1) $2\sqrt{x}$ is an integer
        Therefore, ***x* is a perfect square.**

    (2) $\sqrt{3x}$ is not an integer.

45.   **If $p \times q = 24$, what number is *p*?**
(45.)

    (1) *q* is divisible by 6; thus, *q* equals 24, 12, or 6. ***p* = 1, 2, or 4.**

    (2) *p* is divisible by 2 (OR, *p* is even). ***p* = 2, 4, 6, 8, 12, or 24.**

p	*q*
1	24
2	12
3	8
4	6
6	4
8	3
12	2
24	1

54.   **What is the value of x^{p-q}?**
(53.)

    (1) $p - q = 0$

    (2) $x = 3$

64.   **Is *y* divisible by 3?**
(63.)

    (1)

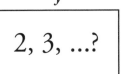

    (2)

78.   **Is p odd?**
(75.)

   (1) p is odd.
   (2) **p is odd.**

79. 2nd Edition only

   $(\text{Any integer})^{\text{positive integer}} = \text{Integer}$ (e.g., 2^5, $(-3)^3$, etc.)

   $(1)^{\text{any power}} = 1 \ (= \text{Integer})$

   Is n a positive integer, or is m equal to 1?

   (1) If n is positive, then m can be any integer (e.g., $2^4 = 16$, $2^{-4} = 1/16$).
      If n is negative, then m must be an even integer (e.g., $(-2)^4 = 16$, $(-2)^{-4} = 1/16$).

   (2) If m is a positive integer, then n can be any integer (e.g., $2^4 = 16$, $(-2)^3 = -8$).
      If $n = 1$, then m can be any integer (e.g., $1^{-2} = 1^7 = 1$).

81.   **Is x a positive proper fraction (a fraction between zero and one)?**
(78.)

   (1) $x < -1$ OR $x > 1$
      x is NOT a positive proper fraction.

   (2) $x > -1$
      x MAY or MAY NOT be a positive proper fraction.

82. 2nd Edition only

   Let n be the original number of books.
   $n \div 10 = \text{integer}$, so $n =$ a multiple of 10 (that is, 10, 20, 30, 40, …)

   $(n + 10) \div 12 = \text{integer}$, so $n + 10 =$ a multiple of 12
   Find multiples of 12 among the multiples of 10.
   $\qquad\qquad n + 10 = 60, 120, 180, 240, \ldots$ (multiples of both 12 and 10)
   $\qquad$ so $\quad n = 50, 110, 170, 230, \ldots$ These are the only possible values of n.

   Which of these numbers (50, 110, 170, etc.) is n?

   (1) $n < 96$
   (2) $n > 24$

86.   **Is $m = n + 1$?**
(82.)

   (1) $m - 1 = (n + 1) + 1$ $\qquad$ OR $\qquad$ $m - 1 = (n + 1) - 1$
      $m - 1 = n + 2$ $\qquad\qquad\qquad\qquad$ $m - 1 = n$
      $m = n + 3$ $\qquad\qquad\qquad\qquad\quad$ $m = n + 1$

Note that $m = n + 3$ contradicts the original question, and is therefore impossible. Discard this possibility. Thus, **$m = n + 1$**.

(2) **m is divisible by 2.**

87. **Is n divisible by 7?**
(83.)

    (1) $n = 2k + 3$

    (2) $2k - 4 = 7x$, where x is an integer

90. There is little rephrasing you can do in this problem. Testing numbers is the best strategy.
(86.)

113. **Is d a perfect square?**
(108.)

    (1) **d is a perfect square.**

    (2) $\sqrt{d}$ is a perfect square; therefore, **d is a perfect square**.

115. **Are there three 2's and one 3 in the prime box for n?**
(110.)

    (1) **There are at least two 2's in the prime box.**

    (2) **There is at least one 2 and at least one 3 in the prime box.**

(111. 1st Edition only)
There is little rephrasing you can do in this problem. Testing numbers is the best strategy.

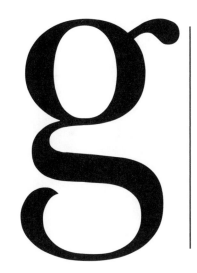

Chapter 9
of
NUMBER PROPERTIES

OFFICIAL GUIDE
PROBLEM SETS:
PART I

In This Chapter . . .

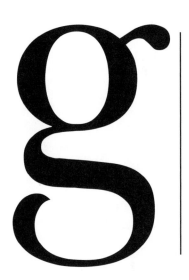

- Number Properties Problem Solving List
  from *The Official Guides:* PART I
- Number Properties Data Sufficiency List
  from *The Official Guides:* PART I

Practicing with REAL GMAT Problems

Now that you have completed Part I of NUMBER PROPERTIES it is time to test your skills on problems that have actually appeared on real GMAT exams over the past several years.

The problem sets that follow are composed of questions from three books published by the Graduate Management Admission Council® (the organization that develops the official GMAT exam):

The Official Guide for GMAT Review, 12th Edition
The Official Guide for GMAT Quantitative Review
The Official Guide for GMAT Quantitative Review, 2nd Edition
Note: The two editions of the Quant Review book largely overlap. Use one OR the other.

These books contain quantitative questions that have appeared on past official GMAT exams. (The questions contained therein are the property of The Graduate Management Admission Council, which is not affiliated in any way with Manhattan GMAT.)

Although the questions in the Official Guides have been "retired" (they will not appear on future official GMAT exams), they are great practice questions.

In order to help you practice effectively, we have categorized every problem in The Official Guides by topic and subtopic. On the following two pages, you will find two categorized lists:

(1) **Problem Solving:** Lists EASIER Problem Solving Number Properties questions contained in *The Official Guides* and categorizes them by subtopic.

(2) **Data Sufficiency:** Lists EASIER Data Sufficiency Number Properties questions contained in *The Official Guides* and categorizes them by subtopic.

The remaining *Official Guide* problems are listed at the end of Part II of this book. **Do not forget about the Part II list!**

Each book in Manhattan GMAT's 8-book strategy series contains its own *Official Guide* lists that pertain to the specific topic of that particular book. If you complete all the practice problems contained on the *Official Guide* lists in each of the 8 Manhattan GMAT strategy books, you will have completed every single question published in *The Official Guides*.

Problem Solving: Part I

from *The Official Guide for GMAT Review, 12th Edition* (pages 20–23 & 152–185), *The Official Guide for GMAT Quantitative Review* (pages 62–85), and *The Official Guide for GMAT Quantitative Review, 2nd Edition* (pages 62–86).

<u>Note</u>: The two editions of the Quant Review book largely overlap. Use one OR the other.

Solve each of the following problems in a notebook, making sure to demonstrate how you arrived at each answer by showing all of your work and computations. If you get stuck on a problem, look back at the NUMBER PROPERTIES strategies and content contained in this guide to assist you.

<u>Note</u>: Problem numbers preceded by "D" refer to questions in the Diagnostic Test chapter of *The Official Guide for GMAT Review, 12th Edition* (pages 20–23).

<u>GENERAL SET – NUMBER PROPERTIES</u>

Divisibility & Primes
> *12th Edition*: 3, 7, 23, 36, 72, 82, 87, 107, 110, 159, D18, D23
> *Quantitative Review*: 98, 102, 103, 109, 122
> OR *2nd Edition*: 78, 98, 109, 122

Odds & Evens
> *12th Edition*: 40

Positives & Negatives
> *12th Edition*: 22, 29, 50
> *Quantitative Review*: 15, 53 OR *2nd Edition*: 17, 55

Consecutive Integers
> *12th Edition*: 85, 116, 157, D2
> *Quantitative Review*: 9 OR *2nd Edition*: 11

Exponents & Roots
> *12th Edition*: 11, 32, 46, 51, 54, 73, 164, D17
> *Quantitative Review*: 34, 45, 64, 81, 97, 117, 145, 147
> OR *2nd Edition*: 36, 47, 86, 97

Remember, there are more Official Guide problems listed at the end of Part II.

Data Sufficiency: Part I

from *The Official Guide for GMAT Review, 12th Edition* (pages 24–26 & 272–288), *The Official Guide for GMAT Quantitative Review* (pages 149–157), and *The Official Guide for GMAT Quantitative Review, 2nd Edition* (pages 152–163).

<u>Note</u>: The two editions of the Quant Review book largely overlap. Use one OR the other.

Solve each of the following problems in a notebook, making sure to demonstrate how you arrived at each answer by showing all of your work and computations. If you get stuck on a problem, look back at the NUMBER PROPERTIES strategies and content contained in this guide to assist you.

Practice REPHRASING both the questions and the statements. The majority of data sufficiency problems can be rephrased; however, if you have difficulty rephrasing a problem, try testing numbers to solve it. It is especially important that you familiarize yourself with the directions for data sufficiency problems, and that you memorize the 5 fixed answer choices that accompany all data sufficiency problems.

<u>Note</u>: Problem numbers preceded by "D" refer to questions in the Diagnostic Test chapter of *The Official Guide for GMAT Review, 12th Edition* (pages 24–26).

GENERAL SET – NUMBER PROPERTIES

Divisibility & Primes
> *12th Edition*: 16, 66, 82, 90, D26, D42
> *Quantitative Review*: 3, 7, 13, 16, 33, 39, 45, 63
> OR *2nd Edition*: 3, 16, 39, 45, 64, 70

Odds & Evens
> *12th Edition*: 6, 12, 17, 24, 73, 76
> *Quantitative Review*: 75 OR *2nd Edition*: 78

Positives & Negatives
> *12th Edition*: 69, 159
> *Quantitative Review*: 76, 94, 101 OR *2nd Edition*: 11, 24, 98, 105

Consecutive Integers
> *12th Edition*: 65, 108
> *Quantitative Review*: 20 OR *2nd Edition*: 20

Exponents & Roots
> *12th Edition*: 169, D44
> *Quantitative Review*: 18, 53, 73, 78, 98
> OR *2nd Edition*: 18, 54, 76, 81

Remember, there are more Official Guide problems listed at the end of Part II.

PART II: ADVANCED

This part of the book covers various advanced topics within *Number Properties*. This advanced material may not be necessary for all students. Attempt Part II only if you have completed Part I and are comfortable with its content.

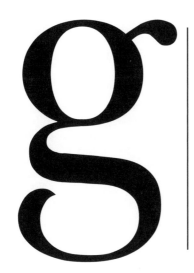

Chapter 10
of
NUMBER PROPERTIES

DIVISIBILITY & PRIMES: ADVANCED

In This Chapter . . .

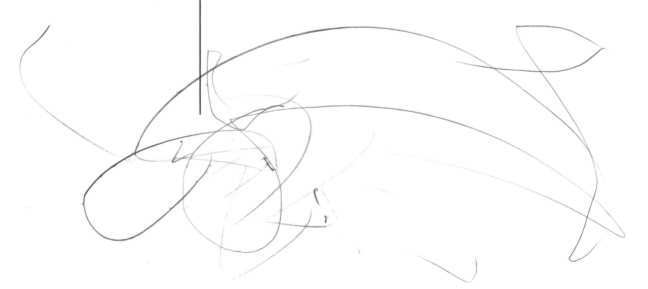

DIVISIBILITY & PRIMES ADVANCED

This chapter covers advanced material within the topic of Divisibility & Primes. From here on out, it is assumed that you have already completed Part I of this book, including the Official Guide problem sets in Chapter 9.

Primes

You should become very comfortable with small prime numbers—at least the first 10. Even better, know (or be able to derive quickly) all the primes up to 100 (2, 3, 5, 7, 11, 13, 17, 19, 23, 29, 31, 37, 41, 43, 47, 53, 59, 61, 67, 71, 73, 79, 83, 89, 97). Here are some additional facts about primes that may be helpful on the GMAT.

(1) **There is an infinite number of prime numbers.** There is no upper limit to the size of prime numbers.

> Do not forget about the only even prime: 2.

(2) **There is no simple pattern in the prime numbers.** Since 2 is the only even prime number, all other primes are odd. However, there is no easy pattern to determining which odd numbers will be prime. Each number needs to be tested directly to determine whether it is prime.

(3) **Positive integers with only two factors must be prime, and positive integers with more than two factors are never prime.** Any integer greater than or equal to 2 has at least two factors: 1 and itself. Thus, if there are only two factors of x (with x equal to an integer ≥ 2), then the factors of x MUST be 1 and x. Therefore, x must be prime. Also, do not forget that the number 1 is NOT prime. The number 1 has only one factor (itself), so it is defined as a non-prime number.

These facts can be used to disguise the topic of prime numbers on the GMAT. Take a look at the following Data Sufficiency examples.

> What is the value of integer x?
>
> (1) x has exactly 2 factors.
> (2) When x is divided by 2, the remainder is 0.

Statement (1) indicates that x is prime, because it has only 2 factors. This statement is insufficient by itself, since there are infinitely many prime numbers. Statement (2) indicates that 2 divides evenly into x, meaning that x is even; that is also insufficient by itself. Taken together, however, the two statements reveal that x must be an even prime—and the only even prime number is 2. The answer is (C): BOTH statements TOGETHER are sufficient, but NEITHER statement ALONE is sufficient.

> If x is a prime number, what is the value of x?
>
> (1) There are a total of 50 prime numbers between 2 and x, inclusive.
> (2) There is no integer n such that x is divisible by n and $1 < n < x$.

At first, this problem seems outlandishly difficult. How are we to list out the first 50 prime numbers in under 2 minutes? Remember, however, that this is a Data Sufficiency problem. We do not need to list the first 50 primes. Instead, all we need to do is determine WHETHER we can do so.

For Statement (1), we know that certain numbers are prime and others are not. We also know that x is prime. Therefore, if we were to list all the primes from 2 on up, we eventually would find the 50th-largest prime number. That number must equal x, because x is prime, so it MUST be the 50th item on that list of primes. This information is SUFFICIENT.

For Statement (2), we are told that x is not divisible by any integer greater than 1 and less than x. Therefore, x can only have 1 and x and factors. In other words, x is prime. We already know this result, in fact: it was given to us in the question stem. So Statement (2) does not help us determine what x is. INSUFFICIENT.

The correct answer is (A): Statement (1) ALONE is sufficient, but statement (2) alone is not sufficient. (Incidentally, for those who are curious, the 50th prime number is 229.)

Divisibility and Addition/Subtraction

We saw in Part I that **if you add or subtract multiples of an integer, you get another multiple of that integer.** We can now generalize to other situations. For the following rules, assume that N is an integer.

> **(1) If you add a multiple of N to a non-multiple of N, the result is a non-multiple of N. (The same holds true for subtraction.)**
> $18 - 10 = 8$ (Multiple of 3) − (Non-multiple of 3) = (Non-multiple of 3)

> **(2) If you add two non-multiples of N, the result could be either a multiple of N or a non-multiple of N.**
> $19 + 13 = 32$ (Non-multiple of 3) + (Non-multiple of 3) = (Non-multiple of 3)
> $19 + 14 = 33$ (Non-multiple of 3) + (Non-multiple of 3) = (Multiple of 3)
> The exception to this rule is when $N = 2$. Two odds always sum to an even.

Try the following Data Sufficiency example.

> Is N divisible by 7?
>
> > (1) $N = x - y$, where x and y are integers
> > (2) x is divisible by 7, and y is not divisible by 7.

Statement (1) tells us that N is the difference between two integers (x and y), but it does not tell us anything about whether x or y is divisible by 7. INSUFFICIENT.

Statement (2) tells us nothing about N. INSUFFICIENT.

Statements (1) and (2) combined tell us that x is a multiple of 7, but y is not a multiple of 7. The difference between x and y can NEVER be divisible by 7 if x is divisible by 7 but y is not. (If you are not convinced, try testing it out by picking numbers.) SUFFICIENT: N cannot be a multiple of 7.

The correct answer is (C): BOTH statements TOGETHER are sufficient, but NEITHER statement ALONE is sufficient.

Advanced GCF and LCM Techniques

While Venn diagrams are helpful for visualizing the steps needed to compute the GCF and LCM, they can be cumbersome if you want to find the GCF or LCM of large numbers or of 3 or more numbers.

FINDING GCF AND LCM USING PRIME COLUMNS

Prime columns is a fast and straightforward technique. Here are the steps:

(1) Calculate the prime factors of each integer.
(2) Create a column for each prime factor found within any of the integers.
(3) Create a row for each integer.
(4) In each cell of the table, place the prime factor raised to a *power*. This power counts how many copies of the column's prime factor appear in the prime box of the row's integer.

To calculate the GCF, take the LOWEST count of each prime factor found across ALL the integers. This counts the **shared primes**. To calculate the LCM, take the HIGHEST count of each prime factor found across ALL the integers. This counts **all the primes less the shared primes**.

Here is an example to demonstrate the method:

> Find the GCF and LCM of 100, 140, and 250.

First, we need to find the prime factorizations of these numbers. $100 = 2 \times 2 \times 5 \times 5 = 2^2 \times 5^2$. $140 = 2 \times 2 \times 5 \times 7 = 2^2 \times 5 \times 7$. Finally, $250 = 2 \times 5 \times 5 \times 5 = 2 \times 5^3$.

Now, set up a table listing the prime factors of each of these integers in exponential notation. The different prime factors are 2, 5, and 7, so we need 3 columns.

Number:	2		5		7
100	2^2	$\times$	5^2	$\times$	$-$
140	2^2	$\times$	5^1	$\times$	7^1
250	2^1	$\times$	5^3		$-$

To calculate the GCF, we take the SMALLEST count (the lowest power) in any column. The reason is that the GCF is formed only out of the SHARED primes (in the overlapping part of the Venn diagram). The smallest count of the factor 2 is **one**, in 250 ($= 2^1 \times 5^3$). The smallest count of the factor 5 is **one**, in 140 ($= 2^2 \times 5^1 \times 7^1$). The smallest count of the factor 7 is **zero**, since 7 does not appear in 100 or in 250. Therefore the GCF is $2^1 \times 5^1 = 10$.

Number:	2		5		7		
100	2^2	$\times$	5^2		$-$		
140	2^2	$\times$	5^1	$\times$	7^1		
250	2^1	$\times$	5^3		$-$		
GCF:	2^1	$\times$	5^1			$=$	$2^1 \times 5^1 = 10$
LCM:	2^2	$\times$	5^3	$\times$	7^1	$=$	$2^2 \times 5^3 \times 7^1 = 3,500$

Use prime columns to calculate the GCF and LCM of 2 or more large numbers quickly.

*Manhattan*GMAT*Prep
the new standard

To calculate the LCM, we take the LARGEST count (the highest power) in any column. The reason is that the LCM is formed out of ALL the primes less the shared primes. The largest count of the factor 2 is **two**, in 140 (= $2^2 \times 5^1 \times 7^1$) and 100 (= $2^2 \times 5^2$). The largest count of the factor 5 is **three**, in 250 (= $2^1 \times 5^3$). The largest count of the factor 7 is **one**, in 140 (= $2^2 \times 5^1 \times 7^1$). Therefore the LCM is $2^2 \times 5^3 \times 7^1 = 3{,}500$.

<u>FINDING GCF AND LCM USING PRIME BOXES OR FACTORIZATIONS</u>
Also, you can use a shortcut directly from the prime boxes or the prime factorizations to find the GCF and LCM. Once you get familiar with the Prime Columns method, you will see that you can just scan the boxes or the factorizations and take all the lowest powers to find the GCF and the highest powers to find the LCM.

What are the GCF and LCM of 30 and 24?

Here is a tip for double-checking your work: for any integers <i>a</i> and <i>b</i>, the GCF times the LCM must equal <i>a</i> × <i>b</i>.

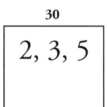

The prime factorization of 30 is $2 \times 3 \times 5$.
The prime factorization of 24 is $2 \times 2 \times 2 \times 3$, or $2^3 \times 3$.
The GCF is $2 \times 3 = 6$.
The LCM is $2^3 \times 3 \times 5 = 120$.

Three general properties of the GCF and LCM are worth noting:

(1) **(GCF of *m* and *n*) × (LCM of *m* and *n*) = *m* × *n*.** The reason for this is that the GCF is composed of the SHARED prime factors of *m* and *n*. The LCM is composed of all of the other, or NON-SHARED, prime factors of *m* and *n*.

(2) **The GCF of *m* and *n* cannot be larger than the difference between *m* and *n*.** For example, assume the GCF of *m* and *n* is 12. Thus, *m* and *n* are both multiples of 12. Consecutive multiples of 12 are 12 units apart on the number line. Therefore, *m* and *n* CANNOT be less than 12 units apart, or else they would not both be multiples of 12.

(3) **Consecutive multiples of *n* have a GCF of *n*.** For example, 8 and 12 are consecutive multiples of 4. Thus 4 is a common factor of both numbers. But 8 and 12 are exactly 4 units apart. Thus 4 is the greatest possible common factor of 8 and 12. (For this reason, the GCF of any two consecutive integers is 1, because both integers are multiples of 1 and the numbers are 1 unit apart.)

Finally, you may be asked to determine what combinations of numbers could lead to a specific GCF or LCM. This is a difficult task. Consider the following problem:

> Is the integer *z* divisible by 6?
>
> > (1) The greatest common factor of *z* and 12 is 3.
> > (2) The greatest common factor of *z* and 15 is 15.

When we calculate the GCF for a set of numbers, we determine the prime factors of each number and then take each prime factor to the LOWEST power it appears in any factorization. In this problem, we are TOLD what the GCF is. We can use the prime columns method to determine what conclusions can be drawn from each of these statements.

Statement (1) tells us that z and 12 ($2 \times 2 \times 3$) have a GCF of 3. Set that information up in a prime columns table to figure out what we can deduce about the prime factors of z.

Notice that the GCF of 12 and z contains a 3. Since the GCF contains each prime factor to the power it appears the LEAST, we know that z must also contain at least one 3. Therefore, z is divisible by 3.

Notice also that the GCF contains NO 2's. Since 12 contains two 2's, z must not contain any 2's. Therefore, z is NOT divisible by 2. Since z is not divisible by 2, it cannot be divisible by 6. SUFFICIENT.

Statement (2) tells us that z and 15 (3×5) have a GCF of 15. We can set that up in a prime columns table to figure out what we can deduce about the prime factors of z:

The GCF of 15 and z contains a 3. Since the GCF contains each prime factor to the power it appears the LEAST, we know that z must also contain at least one 3. Therefore, z is divisible by 3.

Also, the GCF contains a 5. Since the GCF contains each prime factor to the power it appears the LEAST, we know that z must also contain a 5. Therefore, z is divisible by 5.

However, this does NOT tells us whether z contains any 2's. We need z to contain at least one 2 and at least one 3 in its prime factorization for it to be divisible by 6. If z had 2 as a prime factor, 2 would still not be part of the GCF, because 15 has no 2's. Thus we cannot tell whether z has a 2 in its prime factorization. INSUFFICIENT. The correct answer is (A): Statement (1) ALONE is sufficient, but statement (2) alone is not sufficient.

Now consider this example:

> If the LCM of a and 12 is 36, what are the possible values of a?

As in the earlier example, we can use the prime columns technique to draw conclusions about the prime factors of a.

First, notice that a cannot be larger than 36. The LCM of two or more integers is always AT LEAST as large as any of the integers. Therefore the maximum value of a is 36.

Next, notice that the LCM of 12 and a contains two 2's. Since the LCM contains each prime factor to the power it appears the MOST, we know that a cannot contain more than two 2's. It does not necessarily to contain any twos, so a can contain zero, one or two 2's.

Finally, observe that the LCM of 12 and a contains two 3's. But 12 only contains ONE 3. The 3^2 factor in the LCM must have come from the prime factorization of a. Thus we know that a contains exactly two 3's.

Since a must contain exactly two 3's, and can contain no 2's, one 2, or two 2's, a could be $3 \times 3 = 9$, $3 \times 3 \times 2 = 18$, or $3 \times 3 \times 2 \times 2 = 36$. Thus 9, 18, and 36 are the possible values of a.

Other Applications of Primes & Divisibility

COUNTING FACTORS AND PRIMES

The GMAT can ask you to count factors of some number in several different ways. For example, consider the number 1,400. The prime factorization of this number is $2 \times 2 \times 2 \times 5 \times 5 \times 7$, or $2^3 \times 5^2 \times 7$ in **exponential notation**. Here are three different questions that the GMAT could ask you about this integer:

> The GMAT can ask you to calculate the total number of factors, the total number of prime factors (length), or the total number of DIFFERENT prime factors of any integer.

Factors of 1,400 ($2^3 \times 5^2 \times 7$):

(1) How many different prime factors?	**(2) How many total prime factors (length)?**	**(3) How many total factors?**
• May be phrased as "different prime factors" or "unique prime factors" • Count each repeated prime factor only ONCE • In this example, 2, 5, and 7 are distinct, so there are 3 different prime factors	• Length is defined as the number of primes (not necessarily distinct) whose product is x (in this case, whose product is 1,400) • Add the exponents of the prime factors. If there is no exponent, count it as 1. • In this example, the length is $3 + 2 + 1 = 6$.	• Includes all factors, not necessarily just prime factors • Can be determined using "factor pairs" approach, but this is cumbersome for larger numbers • Advanced technique discussed later in this chapter • Do not forget to include 1 as a factor!

Consider the number 252.
(a) How many unique prime factors of 252 are there? Equivalently, how many prime numbers are factors of 252
(b) What is the length of 252 (as defined above)?
(c) How many total factors of 252 are there?

For (a), we can determine the number of unique prime factors by looking at the prime factorization of 252: $2 \times 2 \times 3 \times 3 \times 7$. There are 3 different prime factors in 252: 2, 3, and 7. We do NOT count repeated primes to answer this particular question.

For (b), the "length" of an integer is defined as the total number of primes that, when multiplied together, equal that integer. (Note: on the GMAT, any question that asks about the length of an integer will provide this definition of length, so you do not need to memorize it.) Again we can determine the TOTAL number of prime factors by looking at the prime factorization of 252: $2 \times 2 \times 3 \times 3 \times 7$. There are 5 total prime factors in 252: 2, 2, 3, 3, and 7. In other words, the length of an integer is just the total number of primes in the prime box of that integer. We DO count repeated primes to answer this particular question.

*ManhattanGMAT*Prep
the new standard

You can also answer this question by looking at the prime factorization in exponential form: $252 = 2^2 \times 3^2 \times 7$. Simply add the exponents: $2 + 2 + 1 = 5$. Notice that a number written in this form without an exponent has an **implicit exponent** of 1.

For (c), one way to determine the total number of factors is to determine the factor pairs of 252, using the process described in Part I. Simply start at 1 and "walk up" through all the integers, determining whether each is a factor. Meanwhile, the factors in the large column will naturally get smaller. You can stop once the small column "meets" the large column. For example, since the last entry in the large column is 18, you can stop searching once you have evaluated 17 as a possible factor. Once you have finished, you will notice there are 18 total factors of 252.

Small	Large
1	252
2	126
3	84
4	63
6	42
7	36
9	28
12	21
14	18

This method will be too cumbersome for larger numbers, so a more advanced method is introduced later in this chapter.

Perfect squares always have an odd number of factors; other integers always have an even number of factors.

PERFECT SQUARES, CUBES, ETC.

The GMAT occasionally tests properties of perfect squares, which are squares of other integers. The numbers 4 ($= 2^2$) and 25 ($= 5^2$) are examples of perfect squares. One special property of perfect squares is that **all perfect squares have an odd number of total factors**. Similarly, any integer that has an odd number of total factors MUST be a perfect square. All other non-square integers have an even number of factors. Why is this the case?

Think back to the factor pair exercises we have done so far. Factors come in pairs. If x and y are integers and $x \cdot y = z$, then x and y are a factor pair of z. However, if z is a perfect square, then in *one* of its factor pairs, x equals y. That is, in this particular pair we have $x \cdot x = z$, or $x^2 = z$. This means that we do not have TWO different numbers in this factor "pair." Rather, we have a single unpaired factor: the square root.

Consider the perfect square 36. It has 5 factor pairs that yield 36, as shown to the right. Notice that the FINAL pair is 6 and 6, so instead of $5 \times 2 = 10$ total factors, there are only 9 different factors of 36.

Small	Large
1	36
2	18
3	12
4	9
6	**6**

Notice also that any number that is not a perfect square will NEVER have an odd number of factors. That is because the only way to arrive at an odd number of factors is to have a factor pair in which the two factors are equal.

For larger numbers, it would be much more difficult to use the factor pair technique to prove that a number is a perfect square or that it has an odd number of factors. Thankfully, we can use a different approach. Notice that perfect squares are formed from the product of two copies of the same prime factors. For instance, $90^2 = (2 \times 3^2 \times 5)(2 \times 3^2 \times 5) = 2^2 \times 3^4 \times 5^2$. Therefore, **the prime factorization of a perfect square contains only even powers of primes**. It is also true that any number whose prime factorization contains only even powers of primes must be a perfect square.

Here are some examples.

$$144 = 2^4 \times 3^2 \qquad\qquad 9 = 3^2$$
$$36 = 2^2 \times 3^2 \qquad\qquad 40,000 = 2^6 \times 5^4$$

All of these integers are perfect squares.

By contrast, if a number's prime factorization contains any odd powers of primes, then the number is not a perfect square. For instance, $132,300 = 2^2 \times 3^3 \times 5^2 \times 7^2$ is not a perfect square, because the 3 is raised to an odd power. If this number is multiplied by 3, then the result, 396,900, is a perfect square: $396,900 = 2^2 \times 3^4 \times 5^2 \times 7^2$.

> Prime factors of perfect squares MUST come in pairs; likewise, prime factors of perfect cubes MUST come in groups of 3.

The same logic used for perfect squares extends to perfect cubes and to other "perfect" powers. If a number is a perfect cube, then it is formed from three identical sets of primes, so all the powers of primes are multiples of 3 in the factorization of a perfect cube. For instance, $90^3 = (2 \times 3^2 \times 5)(2 \times 3^2 \times 5)(2 \times 3^2 \times 5) = 2^3 \times 3^6 \times 5^3$.

If k^3 is divisible by 240, what is the least possible value of integer k?
(A) 12   (B) 30   (C) 60   (D) 90   (E) 120

The prime box of k^3 contains the prime factors of 240, which are 2, 2, 2, 2, 3, and 5. We know that the prime factors of k^3 should be the prime factors of k appearing in sets of three, so we should distribute the prime factors of k^3 into three columns to represent the prime factors of k, as shown below.

We see a complete set of three 2's in the prime box of k^3, so k must have a factor of 2. However, there is a fourth 2 left over. That additional factor of 2 must be from k as well, so we assign it to one of the component k columns. We have an incomplete set of 3's in the prime box of k^3, but we can still infer that k has a factor of 3; otherwise k^3 would not have any. Similarly, k^3 has a single 5 in its prime box, but that factor must be one of the factors of k as well. Thus, k has 2, 2, 3, and 5 in its prime box, so k must be a multiple of 60.

Even though we do not initially see them, the factors 2, 3, and 5 must be in these boxes, too. All of the k's must be identical!

The correct answer is **C**.

FACTORIALS AND DIVISIBILITY

The factorial of N, symbolized by $N!$, is the product of all integers from 1 up to and including N. For instance, $6! = 6 \times 5 \times 4 \times 3 \times 2 \times 1 = 720$.

Because it is the product of all the integers from 1 to N, any factorial $N!$ must be divisible by all integers from 1 to N. This follows directly from the Factor Foundation Rule. Another way of saying this is that **$N!$ is a multiple of all the integers from 1 to N.**

This fact works in concert with other properties of divisibility and multiples. For instance, the quantity $10! + 7$ must be a multiple of 7, because both $10!$ and 7 are multiples of 7. $10! + 15$ must be a multiple of 15, because $10!$ is divisible by 5 and 3, and 15 is divisible by 5 and 3. Thus, both numbers are divisible by 15, and the sum is divisible by 15. Finally, $10! + 11!$ is a multiple of any integer from 1 to 10, because every integer between 1 and 10 inclusive is a factor of both $10!$ and $11!$, separately.

Because the factorial $N!$ contains all the integers from 1 up to the number N, it follows that any smaller factorial divides evenly into any larger factorial. For example, $9!$ is divisible by $8!$ or by the factorial of any smaller positive integer. In a quotient of two factorials, the smaller factorial cancels completely. For instance, consider $\dfrac{8!}{5!}$:

$$\frac{8!}{5!} = \frac{8 \cdot 7 \cdot 6 \cdot \cancel{5} \cdot \cancel{4} \cdot \cancel{3} \cdot \cancel{2} \cdot \cancel{1}}{\cancel{5} \cdot \cancel{4} \cdot \cancel{3} \cdot \cancel{2} \cdot \cancel{1}} = 8 \cdot 7 \cdot 6 = 336.$$

$N!$ is the product of all positive integers smaller than or equal to N. Therefore, $N!$ MUST be divisible by all integers from 1 to N.

Advanced Remainders

A remainder is defined as the integer portion of the **dividend** (or numerator) that is not evenly divisible by the **divisor** (or denominator). For example, 23 is not evenly divisible by 4. When you divide 23 by 4, you get a **remainder** of 3 that cannot be divided out, because $23 = 5 \times 4 + 3$. Here is this example written in fractional notation:

$$\text{Dividend} \longrightarrow \frac{23}{4} = 5 + \frac{3}{4} \longleftarrow \text{Remainder}$$
$$\text{Divisor} \longrightarrow \qquad \uparrow \qquad \longleftarrow \text{Quotient}$$

The **quotient** is the resulting integer portion that CAN be divided out (in this case, the quotient is 5). Note that the dividend, divisor, quotient and remainder will ALWAYS be integers. Sometimes, the quotient may be zero! For instance, when 3 is divided by 5, the remainder is 3 (because 0 is the biggest multiple of 5 that can be divided out of 3).

Algebraically, this relationship can be written as:

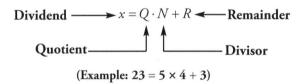

$$\text{Dividend} \longrightarrow \frac{x}{N} = Q + \frac{R}{N} \longleftarrow \text{Remainder}$$
$$\text{Divisor} \longrightarrow \qquad \uparrow \qquad \longleftarrow \text{Quotient}$$

This framework is often easiest to use on GMAT problems when you multiply through by the divisor N:

$$\text{Dividend} \longrightarrow x = Q \cdot N + R \longleftarrow \text{Remainder}$$
$$\text{Quotient} \underline{\qquad} \uparrow \quad \uparrow \underline{\qquad} \text{Divisor}$$

(Example: $23 = 5 \times 4 + 3$)

Again, remember that x, Q, N, and R all must ALL be integers.

CREATING NUMBERS WITH A CERTAIN REMAINDER

Rather than requiring you to find remainders, some GMAT problems require you to generate arbitrary numbers that yield a certain remainder upon division. If you need a number that leaves remainder R upon division by N, simply take any multiple of N and add R to it. This is equivalent to writing $x = Q \times N + R$, since $Q \times N$ is a multiple of N.

For example, if you need a number that leaves a remainder of 5 when divided by 7, you can pick 14 (a multiple of 7) and add 5 to get 19. If you want to write a general algebraic form, you can write $7 \times int + 5$, where *int* represents some random integer. $7 \times int$ is therefore a multiple of 7, and $7 \times int + 5$ is a multiple of 7, plus 5. Consider this example:

> If *x* has a remainder of 3 when divided by 7 and *y* has a remainder of 2 when divided by 7, what is the remainder of *x* + *y* when divided by 7?

> In a remainder problem, the dividend, divisor, quotient, and remainder must ALL be integers.

One way to solve this problem is simply to pick suitable numbers for x and y. For example, $14 + 3 = 17$ could be x, and $7 + 2 = 9$ could be y. Adding them together, we see that $17 + 9 = 26$, which has a remainder of 5 when divided by 7. In shorthand, we can write R3 + R2 = R5. Algebraically, you could solve this problem by writing $x = 7 \times int_1 + 3$ and $y = 7 \times int_2 + 2$. (The two int's are not necessarily the same, so we have put subscripts 1 and 2 on them.) Then $x + y = 7 \times int_1 + 3 + 7 \times int_2 + 2$, which equals $7 \times (int_1 + int_2) + 3 + 2$, which equals a multiple of 7, plus 5. Thus the remainder is 5. Notice that this remainder is the sum of the remainders of x and y.

VISUALIZING REMAINDERS

We can visualize the problem above by constructing a "Remainder Ruler"—a number line marked off with large and small tick marks. The large tick marks are for the multiples we care about—in this case, multiples of 7. The small tick marks are for all the other integers.

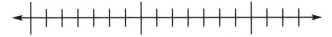

Numbers that leave a remainder of 2 after division by 7 are located two small ticks to the right of a large tick. This is because such numbers are equal to a multiple of 7, plus 2:

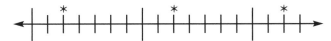

Likewise, numbers that leave a remainder of 3 after division by 7 are located three small ticks to the right of a large tick.

So, when you add a number with 2 extra small ticks to a number with 3 extra small ticks, you get 5 extra small ticks.

RANGE OF POSSIBLE REMAINDERS

When you divide an integer by 7, the remainder could be 0, 1, 2, 3, 4, 5, or 6. Notice that you cannot have a negative remainder or a remainder larger than 7, and that you have exactly 7 possible remainders. You can see these remainders repeating themselves on the Remainder Ruler:

This pattern can be generalized. When you divide an integer by a positive integer N, the possible remainders range from 0 to $(N - 1)$. There are thus N possible remainders. Negative remainders are not possible, nor are remainders equal to or larger than N.

> The remainder of any number MUST be non-negative and smaller than the divisor.

> If $a \div b$ yields a remainder of 5, $c \div d$ yields a remainder of 8, and a, b, c and d are all integers, what is the smallest possible value for $b + d$?

Since the remainder must be smaller than the divisor, 5 must be smaller than b. b must be an integer, so b is at least 6. Similarly, 8 must be smaller than d, and d must be an integer, so d must be at least 9. Therefore the smallest possible value for $b + d$ is $6 + 9 = 15$.

<u>REMAINDER OF 0</u>

If x divided by y yields a remainder of 0 (commonly referred to as "no remainder"), then x is divisible by y. Conversely, if x is divisible by y, then x divided by y yields a remainder of 0 (or "no remainder").

Similarly, if x divided by y yields a remainder greater than 0, then x is NOT divisible by y, and vice versa.

<u>ARITHMETIC WITH REMAINDERS</u>

Two useful tips for arithmetic with remainders, if you have the same divisor throughout:

(1) **You can add and subtract remainders directly, as long as you correct excess or negative remainders.** "Excess remainders" are remainders larger than or equal to the divisor. To correct excess or negative remainders, just add or subtract the divisor. For instance, if x leaves a remainder of 4 after division by 7, and y leaves a remainder of 2 after division by 7, then $x + y$ leaves a remainder of $4 + 2 = 6$ after division by 7. You do not need to pick numbers or write algebraic expressions for x and y. We can simply write R4 + R2 = R6.

If x leaves a remainder of 4 after division by 7 and z leaves a remainder of 5 after division by 7, then adding the remainders together yields 9. This number is too high, however. The remainder must be non-negative and less than 7. We can take an additional 7 out of the remainder, because 7 is the **excess** portion. Thus $x + z$ leaves a remainder of $9 - 7 = 2$ after division by 7. We can write R4 + R5 = R9 = R2 (taking out the excess 7). Algebraically, we can write $x = 7 \times int_1 + 4$ and $z = 7 \times int_2 + 5$. Then $x + z = 7 \times int_1 + 4 + 7 \times int_2 + 5 = 7 \times (int_1 + int_2) + 9 = 7 \times (int_1 + int_2) + 7 + 2$. Now, most of that expression, $7 \times (int_1 + int_2) + 7$, represents just another multiple of 7, so we can say that $x + z$ is a multiple of 7, plus 2.

With the same x and z, subtraction of the remainders gives -1, which is also an unacceptable remainder (it must be non-negative). In this case, add an extra 7 to see that $x - z$ leaves a remainder of 6 after division by 7. Using R's, we can write R4 - R5 = R(-1) = R6 (adding a 7 in). To prove this algebraically, we can write $x = 7 \times int_1 + 4$ and $z = 7 \times int_2 + 5$. Then $x - z = 7 \times int_1 + 4 - (7 \times int_2 + 5) = 7 \times (int_1 - int_2) - 1 = 7 \times (int_1 - int_2 - 1) + 7 - 1 = 7 \times (int_1 - int_2 - 1) + 6$, so $x - z$ is a multiple of 7, plus 6. Notice that the algebra is a far more painful method!

Of course, you can often pick numbers to solve problems with remainders. Let us pick $x = 25$ and $z = 12$:

$$25 + 12 = 37 = 5 \cdot 7 + 2 \longleftarrow \text{Remainder}$$

Quotient ———— ⤒ ⤒ ———— Divisor

$$25 - 12 = 13 = 1 \cdot 7 + 6 \longleftarrow \text{Remainder}$$

Quotient ———— ⤒ ⤒ ———— Divisor

(2) You can multiply remainders, as long as you correct excess remainders at the end.

Again, if x has a remainder of 4 upon division by 7 and z has a remainder of 5 upon division by 7, then 4×5 gives 20. Two additional 7's can be taken out of this remainder, so $x \cdot z$ will have remainder 6 upon division by 7. In other words, (R4)(R5) = R20 = R6 (taking out two 7's). We can prove this by again picking $x = 25$ and $z = 12$ (try the algebraic method on your own!):

$$25 \times 12 = 300 = 42 \cdot 7 + 6 \longleftarrow \text{Remainder}$$

Quotient ———— ⤒ ⤒ ———— Divisor

REMAINDERS AND DECIMALS

We say that 17 is not divisible by 5, because it leaves a remainder of 2 after division by 5. However, if you punch "17 ÷ 5 =" into a calculator, it gives you a number back: 3.4. This quotient has an integer portion (3) and a decimal portion (0.4). The decimal portion represents the remainder 2 divided by 5, as shown below.

$$\frac{17}{5} = 3.4 = 3 + \frac{2}{5} \qquad \text{In other words, } 0.4 = \frac{2}{5}, \text{ or Decimal Part} = \frac{\text{Remainder}}{\text{Divisor}}$$

We can use this relationship to solve remainder problems that involve decimals.

> When positive integer A is divided by positive integer B, the result is 4.35.
> Which of the following could be the remainder when A is divided by B?
>
> (A) 13   (B) 14   (C) 15   (D) 16   (E) 17

We isolate the decimal part of the division result: 0.35. Now we set that decimal equal to the unknown remainder R divided by the divisor B:

$$0.35 = \frac{\text{Remainder}}{\text{Divisor}} = \frac{R}{B}$$

Now, express the decimal as a fraction and reduce: $0.35 = \dfrac{35}{100} = \dfrac{7}{20} = \dfrac{R}{B}$

Finally, we cross-multiply: $7B = 20R$

Now, since both B and R are integers, we can see that R must contain a 7 in its prime factorization; otherwise, there is no way for a 7 to appear on the left side. Thus, R must be a multiple of 7. The only answer choice that is a multiple of 7 is 14, which is the correct answer.

The decimal part of a quotient equals the remainder divided by the divisor.

Counting Total Factors

We have discussed using the **factor pair** method to determine the number of total factors of an integer. The problem with this method is that it is slow, tedious, and prone to error. These problems are compounded when the number being analyzed has a large number of factors. Therefore, we need a general method to apply to more difficult problems of this type.

> How many different factors does 2,000 have?

It would take a very long time to list all of the factors of 2,000. However, prime factorization can shorten the process considerably. First, factor 2,000 into primes: $2,000 = 2^4 \times 5^3$. The key to this method is to consider each distinct prime factor separately.

Consider the prime factor 2 first. Because the prime factorization of 2,000 contains four 2's, there are **five possibilities for the number of 2's** in any factor of 2,000: none, one, two, three, or four. (Do not forget the possibility of NO occurrences! For example, 5 is a factor of 2,000, and 5 does not have ANY 2's in its prime box.)

Next, consider the prime factor 5. There are three 5's, so there are **four possibilities for the number of 5's** in a factor of 2,000: none, one, two, or three. (Again, do not forget the possibility of NO occurrences of 5.) Any number with more than four 2's in its prime box cannot be a factor of 2,000.

In general, if a prime factor appears to the Nth power, then there are $(N + 1)$ possibilities for the occurrences of that prime factor. This is true for each of the individual prime factors of any number.

We can borrow a principle from the field of combinatorics called the **Fundamental Counting Principle** to simplify the calculation of the number of prime factors in 2,000. The Fundamental Counting Principle states that if you must make a number of separate decisions, then MULTIPLY the numbers of ways to make each *individual* decision to find the number of ways to make *all* the decisions. (For an elaboration of this principle, see the "Combinatorics" chapter of Manhattan GMAT's *Word Translations* Strategy Guide.)

The number of 2's and the number of 5's to include in a factor of 2,000 are two individual decisions we must make. These two choices are INDEPENDENT of one another, so the total number of factors of 2,000 must be $(4 + 1)(3 + 1) = 5 \times 4 = 20$ different factors.

The logic behind this process can also be represented in the following table of factors. (Note that there is no reason to make this table, unless you are interested in the specific factors themselves. It simply illustrates the reasoning behind multiplying the possibilities.)

	2^0	2^1	2^2	2^3	2^4
5^0	1	2	4	8	16
5^1	5	10	20	40	80
5^2	25	50	100	200	400
5^3	125	250	500	1,000	2,000

Some basic combinatorics theory can help streamline the process of counting factors for any integer.

Each entry in the table is the unique product of a power of 2 (the columns) and a power of 5 (the rows). For instance, $50 = 2^1 \times 5^2$. Notice that the factor in the top left corner contains no 5's and no 2's. That factor is 1 (which equals $2^0 \times 5^0$).

We can easily see that the table has 5 columns (representing the possible power of 2 in the factor) and 4 rows (representing the possible power of 5 in the factor). Thus, the total number of factors is given by 5 columns × 4 rows = 20 different factors.

Although a table like the one above cannot be easily set up for more than two prime factors, the process can be generalized to numbers with more than two prime factors. If a number has prime factorization $a^x \times b^y \times c^z$ (where a, b, and c are all prime), then the number has $(x + 1)(y + 1)(z + 1)$ different factors.

For instance, $9,450 = 2^1 \times 3^3 \times 5^2 \times 7^1$, so 9,450 has $(1 + 1)(3 + 1)(2 + 1)(1 + 1) = 48$ different factors.

Do not forget to add 1 to each exponent when you multiply exponents together to count factors!

Problem Set (Advanced)

1.   If w is a prime number greater than 3, and $z = 36w$, what is the least common multiple of z and $6w$, in terms of w?

2.   If $y = 30p$, and p is prime, what is the greatest common factor of y and $14p$, in terms of p?

3. a, b and c are positive integers greater than 1. If $a < b < c$ and $abc = 286$, what is $c - b$?

4.   If z is an integer and $z!$ is divisible by 340, what is the smallest possible value for z?

5.   All of the following have the same set of unique prime factors EXCEPT:

      (A) 420   (B) 490   (C) 560   (D) 700   (E) 980

6.   Which of the following numbers has exactly 15 factors?

      (A) 105   (B) 108   (C) 120   (D) 144   (E) 168

Solve Data Sufficiency Problems #7–14:

7.   Is p divisible by 168?
         (1) p is divisible by 14
         (2) p is divisible by 12

8.   Is pq divisible by 168?
         (1) p is divisible by 14
         (2) q is divisible by 12

9.   Is the sum of integers a and b divisible by 7?
         (1) a is not divisible by 7.
         (2) b is not divisible by 7.

10.   Is the sum of integers a and b divisible by 7?
         (1) a is not divisible by 7.
         (2) $a - b$ is divisible by 7.

11.   What is the greatest common factor of x and y?
         (1) x and y are both divisible by 4.
         (2) $x - y = 4$

12.   Is x divisible by 120?
         (1) x is divisible by 12.
         (2) x is divisible by 30.

13.   Is x divisible by 8?
         (1) x is divisible by 24.
         (2) x is not divisible by 16.

*Manhattan*GMAT*Prep

14.   What is the value of integer x?
    (1) The least common multiple of x and 45 is 225.
    (2) The least common multiple of x and 20 is 300.

Solve Problems #15–18:

15.   If x^2 is divisible by 216, what is the smallest possible value for positive integer x?

16.   If $x = 1,350$:
    (a) How many distinct prime factors does x have?
    (b) How many total prime factors does x have? (In other words, what is the length of x?)
    (c) How many total factors does x have?

17.   What is the maximum possible length of an integer less than 600? (The length of an integer is the total number of prime factors in its prime factorization.)

18.   Which of the following numbers is NOT prime? (Hint: avoid actually computing these numbers.)

    (A) $6! - 1$ (B) $6! + 21$ (C) $6! + 41$ (D) $7! - 1$ (E) $7! + 11$

For problems #19–23, integer x has a remainder of 5 when divided by 9, and integer y has a remainder of 7 when divided by 9.

19.   What is the remainder when $x + y$ is divided by 9?

20.   What is the remainder when $x - y$ is divided by 9?

21.   What is the remainder when $y - x$ is divided by 9?

22.   What is the remainder when $x \cdot y$ is divided by 9?

23.   What is the remainder when $5x - y$ is divided by 9?

Solve problems #24–26:

24.   If x and y are positive integers and $x \div y$ has a remainder of 5, what is the smallest possible value of xy?

25. a and b are integers such that $\dfrac{a}{b} = 3.45$. If R is the remainder of $\dfrac{a}{b}$, which of the following could NOT be equal to R?

    (A) 3   (B) 9   (C) 36   (D) 81   (E) 144

26.   When 15 is divided by y, the remainder is $y - 3$. If y must be an integer, what are all the possible values of y?

*Manhattan*GMAT Prep
the new standard

1. $36w$:

Number:	2	3	w
$36w$	2^2 $\times$	3^2 $\times$	w^1
$6w$	2^1 $\times$	3^1 $\times$	w^1
LCM:	$\mathbf{2^2}$ $\times$	$\mathbf{3^2}$ $\times$	$\mathbf{w^1}$

Even though we do not know which prime number w is, we can set up a column for it and proceed normally. Since $z = 36w$, the least common multiple of z and $6w$ is the least common multiple of $36w$ and $6w$.

$36w = 2 \times 2 \times 3 \times 3 \times w.$ $6w = 2 \times 3 \times w.$

The least common multiple is the product of all the factors of both integers, using the higher power of repeated factors: (2^2 instead of 2^1 and 3^2 instead of 3^1). $2^2 \times 3^2 \times w = 2 \times 2 \times 3 \times 3 \times w = 36w.$

Notice that it is not actually necessary for w to be a prime number larger than 3. As long as w is a positive integer, the same answer will hold true: the LCM of $6w$ and $36w$ is $36w$.

2. $2p$:

Number:	2	3	5	7	p
$30p$	2^1 $\times$	3^1 $\times$	5^1	$-$ $\times$	p^1
$14p$	2^1	$-$	$-$ $\times$	7^1 $\times$	p^1
GCF:	$\mathbf{2^1}$			$-$ $\times$	$\mathbf{p^1}$

The greatest common factor of y (= $30p$) and $14p$ is the product of all the common prime factors, using the lower power of repeated factors. The only repeated factors are 2 and p: $2^1 \times p^1 = 2 \times p = 2p$. Again, we would get the same answer if p were any positive integer.

3. **2:** We do not know the values of a, b, and c individually, but we do know that a, b, and c are positive integers greater than 1, and that the product of a, b, and c equals 286. Therefore, we should take the prime factorization of 286: $286 = 143 \times 2 = 13 \times 11 \times 2$. There are a total of 3 integers in this product. Furthermore, a, b, and c must each be larger than one. Thus one of the prime factors must equal a, one of the prime factors must equal b, and one of the prime factors must equal c.

We know from the problem that $a < b < c$, so a must equal 2, b must equal 11, and c must equal 13. $c - b$ is therefore equal to $13 - 11 = 2$.

4. **17:** In order for $z!$ to be divisible by 340, it must be divisible by all of the prime factors of 340. The prime factorization of 340 is as follows:

$$340 = 10 \times 34 = 2 \times 5 \times 2 \times 17$$

In order for $z!$ to be divisible by 2, z must be at least 2. In order for $z!$ to be divisible by 2×2, z must be at least 4. ($4! = 4 \times 3 \times 2 \times 1 = \mathbf{2 \times 2} \times 3 \times 2 \times 1$). In order for $z!$ to be divisible by 5, z must be at least 5. And finally, in order for $z!$ to be divisible by 17, z must be at least 17. Thus, z must be at least 17.

5. **(A) 420:** To solve this problem, take the prime factorization of each answer choice and note the unique prime factors. One of the answer choices will have a different set of unique prime factors than the other answer choices.

     (A) 420 = $42 \times 10 = 21 \times 2 \times 2 \times 5 = \mathbf{3} \times 7 \times 2 \times 2 \times 5$. **(Unique primes: 2, 3, 5, and 7.)**
     (B) 490 = $49 \times 10 = 7 \times 7 \times 2 \times 5$ (Unique primes: 2, 5, and 7.)
     (C) 560 = $56 \times 10 = 7 \times 8 \times 2 \times 5 = 7 \times 2 \times 2 \times 2 \times 2 \times 5$. (Unique primes: 2, 5, and 7.)
     (D) 700 = $70 \times 10 = 7 \times 2 \times 5 \times 2 \times 5$ (Unique primes: 2, 5, and 7.)
     (E) 980 = $98 \times 10 = 49 \times 2 \times 2 \times 5 = 7 \times 7 \times 2 \times 2 \times 5$. (Unique primes: 2, 5, and 7.)

The correct answer is (A), because it is the only answer choice with a prime factor of 3.

6. **(D) 144:** This problem can be solved by enumerating the factor pairs of each answer choice to determine which number has exactly 15 factors. Alternatively, you could calculate the prime factorization of each answer choice and write them in exponential notation. Add 1 to all of the exponents and multiply to determine the number of factors.

However, first we should eliminate ALL answer choices that are not perfect squares. Why? **Because only perfect squares have an odd number of factors, and 15 is odd.** As it turns out, only (D) is a perfect square. Therefore only (D) can possibly have exactly 15 factors. Indeed, 144 has 15 factors: 1, 2, 3, 4, 6, 8, 9, 12, 16, 18, 24, 36, 48, 96, and 144.

7. **(E):** The first step in this kind of problem is to determine what prime factors p needs in order to be divisible by 168. The prime factorization of 168 is $2 \times 2 \times 2 \times 3 \times 7$, so the question can be restated as follows:

168

$$2, 2, 2, \\ 3, 7$$

Are there at least three 2's, one 3, and one 7 in the prime box of p?

Statement (1) tells us that p is divisible by 14, which is 2×7. Therefore, we know that p has at least a 2 and a 7 in its prime box. However, we do not know anything else about the possible prime factors in p, so we cannot determine whether p is divisible by 168. For example, p could equal $2 \times 2 \times 2 \times 3 \times 7 = 168$, in which case the answer to the question is "yes, p is divisible by 168." Alternatively, p could equal $2 \times 7 = 14$, in which case the answer to the question is "no, p is NOT divisible by 168." Therefore Statement (1) is insufficient.

Statement (1): p

$$2, 7, \\ \dots?$$

Statement (2) tells us that p is divisible by 12, which is $2 \times 2 \times 3$. Therefore, we know that p has at least two 2's and a 3 in its prime box. However, we do not know anything else about p, so we cannot determine whether p is divisible by 168. For example, p could equal 168, in which case the answer to the question is "yes, p is divisible by 168." Alternatively, p could equal 12, in which case the answer to the question is "no, p is NOT divisible by 168." Statement (2) is insufficient.

Statement (2): p

$$2, 2, 3, \\ \dots?$$

What about combining the information from Statements (1) and (2)? Can we simply take all of the primes from the two prime boxes we created, put them into a new prime box, and determine whether p is divisible by 168? Combining the primes from Statements (1) and (2), we *seem* to have three 2's, a 3, and a 7. That should be sufficient to prove that p is divisible by 168.

INCORRECT:
Stmt's (1) & (2): p

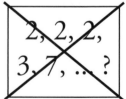

The short answer is no, we cannot do this. Consider the number 84. 84 is divisible by 14. It is also divisible by 12. Therefore, following from Statements (1) and (2), p could be 84. However, 84 is not divisible by 168. $84 = 2 \times 2 \times 3 \times 7$, so we are missing a needed 2.

BOTH statements mention that p contains at least one 2 in its prime factorization. It is possible that these statements are referring to the SAME 2. Therefore, one of the 2's in Statement (2) OVERLAPS with the 2 from Statement (1). You have been given REDUNDANT information. The two boxes you made for Statements (1) and (2) are not truly different boxes. Rather, they are two different views of the same box (the prime box of p).

Thus, we have to eliminate the redundant 2 when we combine the two views of p's prime box from Statements (1) and (2). Given both statements, we only know that p has two 2's, a 3, and a 7 in its prime box. INSUFFICIENT. The correct answer is (E): Statements (1) and (2) TOGETHER are NOT sufficient.

CORRECT:
Stmt's (1) & (2): p

$$2, 2, \\ 3, 7, ... ?$$

8. **(C):** The information in the two statements is NOT redundant. There is no overlap between the prime boxes, because the prime boxes belong to different variables (p and q). Statement (1) tells us that p has at least one 2 and one 7 in its prime box. Statement (2) tells us that q has at least two 2's and one 3 in its prime box. When we combine the two statements, we combine the prime boxes without removing any overlap, because there is no such overlap. As a result, we know that the product pq contains at least THREE 2's, one 3, and one 7 in its combined prime box. We can now answer the question "Is pq divisible by 168?" with a definitive "Yes," since the question is really asking whether pq contains at least three 2's, one 3, and one 7 in its prime box.

The correct answer to this problem is (C): Statements (1) and (2) TOGETHER are SUFFICIENT.

9. **(E):** We need to determine whether $a + b$ is divisible by 7. Statement (1) tells us that a is not divisible by 7, but does not tell us anything about b. NOT SUFFICIENT. Statement (2) tells us that b is not divisible by 7, but does not tell us anything about a. Again, this is NOT SUFFICIENT.

Statements (1) and (2) combined tell us that NEITHER a nor b is divisible by 7. Therefore it is possible that $a + b$ is divisible by 7, but also possible that $a + b$ is NOT divisible by 7. For example, if $a = 4$ and $b = 10$, then $a + b = 14$, which is divisible by 7. However, if $a = 4$ and $b = 11$, then $a + b = 15$, which is NOT divisible by 7. NOT SUFFICIENT. The correct answer is (E): Statements (1) and (2) together are NOT sufficient.

10. **(C):** We need to determine whether $a + b$ is divisible by 7. Statement (1) tells us that a is not divisible by 7, but does not tell us anything about b. NOT SUFFICIENT.

Statement (2) tells us that $a - b$ is divisible by 7. This is not enough information to answer the question. It is possible that $a + b$ is divisible by 7. For example, if $a = 21$ and $b = 14$ then $a - b = 7$, which is divisible by 7, and $a + b = 35$, which is divisible by 7. However, if $a = 20$ and $b = 13$ then $a - b = 7$, which is divisible by 7, but $a + b = 33$, which is NOT divisible by 7. This is NOT SUFFICIENT.
Statements (1) and (2) combined tell us that a is not divisible by 7, but $a - b$ is divisible by 7. This tells us that a and b have the SAME REMAINDER when divided by 7: if $a - b$ is divisible by 7, then the remainder of $a - b$ is zero. Therefore, the remainders of a and b must be equal.

Again, we know that a is not divisible by 7. Therefore, the remainder of a divided by 7 is nonzero. We can test different remainders for a (which must be equal to the remainder for b) and see whether the remainder of $a + b$ can be zero (in other words, let us see whether $a + b$ can be divisible by 7):

Remainder of a	Remainder of b	Remainder of $a + b$
1	1	$1 + 1 = 2$
2	2	$2 + 2 = 4$
3	3	$3 + 3 = 6$
4	4	$4 + 4 = 8 \longrightarrow 1$
5	5	$5 + 5 = 10 \longrightarrow 3$
6	6	$6 + 6 = 12 \longrightarrow 5$

No matter what remainder we choose for a, $a + b$ will not have a remainder of 0, and therefore cannot be divisible by 7. SUFFICIENT. The correct answer is (C): BOTH statements TOGETHER are sufficient, but NEITHER statement ALONE is sufficient.

11. **(C):** Statement (1) tells us that x and y are both divisible by 4, but that does not tell us the GCF of x and y. For example, if $x = 16$ and $y = 20$, then the GCF is 4. However, if $x = 16$ and $y = 32$, then the GCF is 16. NOT SUFFICIENT.

Statement (2) tells us that $x - y = 4$, but that does not tell us the GCF of x and y. For example, if $x = 1$ and $y = 5$, then the GCF is 1. However, if $x = 16$ and $y = 20$, then the GCF is 4. NOT SUFFICIENT.

Combined, Statements (1) and (2) tell us that x and y are multiples of 4 and that they are 4 apart on the number line. Therefore, **x and y are consecutive multiples of 4**. In the GCF/LCM section of this chapter, we explained the following property of greatest common factors: **Consecutive multiples of n have a GCF of n**. Since x and y are consecutive multiples of 4, their GCF equals 4. SUFFICIENT. The correct answer is (C): BOTH statements TOGETHER are sufficient, but NEITHER statement ALONE is sufficient.

12. **(E):** $120 = 2 \times 2 \times 2 \times 3 \times 5$. Therefore to answer this question, we need to know whether x has three 2's, a 3, and a 5 in its prime box.

Statement (1): x   **Statement (2): x**   **Stmt's (1) & (2): x**

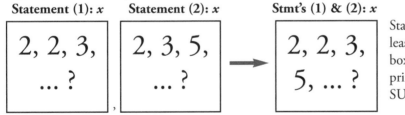

Statement (1) tells us that x has at least two 2's and a 3 in its prime box. We are missing two needed primes: a 2 and a 5. NOT SUFFICIENT.

Statement (2) tells us that x has at least a 2, a 3, and a 5 in its prime box. We are missing two primes: two more 2's are needed. NOT SUFFICIENT.

Combining these statements, only TWO 2's are definitely in the prime factorization of x, because the 2 in the prime factorization of 30 may be REDUNDANT—that is, it may be the SAME 2 as one of the 2's in the prime factorization of 12. We are still missing a needed 2. NOT SUFFICIENT. The correct answer is (E): Statements (1) and (2) together are NOT sufficient.

If you need more proof that we cannot determine whether x is divisible by 120, consider 60. The number 60 is divisible by both 12 and 30. However, it is NOT divisible by 120. Therefore, x could equal 60, in which case it is not divisible by 120. Alternatively, x could equal 120, in which case it IS divisible by 60.

13. (A): $8 = 2 \times 2 \times 2$. Therefore to answer this question, we need to know whether x has three 2's in its prime box.

Statement (1): x

$$2, 2, 2, 3, \; ... \, ?$$

Statement (2): x

$$(\text{not } 2, 2, 2, \text{ and } 2)$$

Statement (1) tells us that x has at least three 2's and a 3 in its prime box. We only need three 2's, so the 3 is superfluous. x MUST be divisible by 8. SUFFICIENT.

Statement (2) tells us that x does NOT have four 2's in its prime box. However, it is still possible that x has three 2's. For example, 24 has three 2's in its prime factorization, but not four 2's. Thus x **might be** divisible by 8, but it **does not have to be** divisible by 8. NOT SUFFICIENT.

The correct answer is (A): Statement (1) ALONE is sufficient, but Statement (2) alone is NOT sufficient.

14. (C): We will try to determine the value of x using the LCM of x and certain other integers.

Statement (1) tells us that x and 45 ($3 \times 3 \times 5$) have an LCM of 225 ($= 3 \times 3 \times 5 \times 5 = 3^2 \times 5^2$).

Number:	3		5
x	?	$\times$	?
45	3^2	$\times$	5^1
LCM:	3^2	$\times$	5^2

Notice that the LCM of x and 45 contains two 3's. 45 contains two 3's, so x can contain zero, one, or two 3's. The LCM of x and 45 contains two 5's. 45 contains only ONE 5, so x must contain **exactly** two 5's. (If x contained more 5's, the LCM would contain more 5's. If x contained fewer 5's, the LCM would contain fewer 5's.)

Therefore x can be any of the following numbers:

$$x = 5 \times 5 = 25$$
$$x = 3 \times 5 \times 5 = 75$$
$$x = 3 \times 3 \times 5 \times 5 = 225$$

NOT SUFFICIENT.

Statement (2) tells us that x and 20 ($2 \times 2 \times 5$) have an LCM of 300 ($= 2 \times 2 \times 3 \times 5 \times 5 = 2^2 \times 3^1 \times 5^2$).

Number:	2		3		5
x	?	$\times$	?	$\times$	?
20	2^2		–	$\times$	5^1
LCM:	2^2	$\times$	3^1	$\times$	5^2

The LCM of x and 20 contains two 2's. 20 contains two 3's, so x can contain zero, one, or two 2's. The LCM of x and 20 contains one 3. 20 contains NO 3's, so x must contain **exactly** one 3.

Furthermore, the LCM of x and 20 contains two 5's. 20 contains one 5, so x must contain **exactly** two 5's.

Therefore x can be any of the following numbers:

$x = 3 \times 5 \times 5 = 75$.
$x = 2 \times 3 \times 5 \times 5 = 150$.
$x = 2 \times 2 \times 3 \times 5 \times 5 = 300$.

NOT SUFFICIENT.

From the two statements combined, we know that $x = 25$, 75, or 225 (Statement (1) tells us this). Also we know that $x = 75$, 150, or 300 (Statement (2) tells us this). The only number that satisfies both of these conditions is $x = 75$. Therefore, we know that x must be 75. SUFFICIENT. The correct answer is (C): BOTH statements TOGETHER are sufficient, but NEITHER statement ALONE is sufficient.

15. **36:** The prime box of x^2 contains the prime factors of 216, which are 2, 2, 2, 3, 3, and 3. We know that the prime factors of x^2 should be the prime factors of x appearing in sets of two, or pairs. Therefore, we should distribute the prime factors of x^2 into two columns to represent the prime factors of x, as shown to the right.

We see a complete pair of two 2's in the prime box of x^2, so x must have a factor of 2. However, there is a third 2 left over. That additional factor of 2 must be from x as well, so we assign it to one of the component x columns. Also, we see a complete pair of two 3's in the prime box of x^2, so x must have a factor of 3. However, there is a third 3 left over. That additional factor of 3 must be from x as well, so we assign it to one of the component x columns. Thus, x has 2, 3, 2, and 3 in its prime box, so x must be a positive multiple of 36.

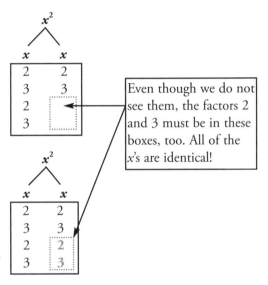

Even though we do not see them, the factors 2 and 3 must be in these boxes, too. All of the x's are identical!

16. **(a) 3:** For this problem, we must find the prime factorization of x. It will be helpful to write it in exponential notation when we are finished:

$1{,}350 = 135 \times 10 = 27 \times 5 \times 5 \times 2 = 3 \times 3 \times 3 \times 5 \times 5 \times 2$. In exponential notation, this equals $2^1 \times 3^3 \times 5^2$.

The distinct prime factors of 1,350 are 2, 3, and 5. Therefore, x has 3 distinct prime factors.

(b) 6: The total prime factors of x is 6: one 2, three 3's, and two 5's. You can also add the exponents in the exponential notation of the prime factorization. $1{,}350 = 2^1 \times 3^3 \times 5^2$, so $1 + 3 + 2 = 6$.

(c) 24: Now that we have written the prime factorization of 1,350 in exponential notation, we can apply the shortcut for calculating the number of total factors of an integer (discussed earlier in this chapter): simply take the exponents on each prime factor, add 1 to each, and multiply them all together. $1{,}350 = 2^1 \times 3^3 \times 5^2$, so $(1 + 1)(3 + 1)(2 + 1) = 2 \times 4 \times 3 = 24$.

We could also compute the number of factors using the factor pairs approach, but this process would be cumbersome and it would be easy to miss a factor pair, because 1,350 is a large number and has many factors.

17. **9:** To maximize the length of an integer of any given size, we want to pick the smallest factors possible. Therefore we should use the smallest possible prime factors (that is, 2's) to get the maximum possible length:

$2 \times 2 = 4$ (Length of 2)
$2 \times 2 \times 2 = 8$ (Length of 3)

$2 \times 2 \times 2 \times 2 = 16$	(Length of 4)
$2 \times 2 \times 2 \times 2 \times 2 = 32$	(Length of 5)
$2 \times 2 \times 2 \times 2 \times 2 \times 2 = 64$	(Length of 6)
$2 \times 2 \times 2 \times 2 \times 2 \times 2 \times 2 = 128$	(Length of 7)
$2 \times 2 \times 2 \times 2 \times 2 \times 2 \times 2 \times 2 = 256$	(Length of 8)
$2 \times 2 \times 2 \times 2 \times 2 \times 2 \times 2 \times 2 \times 2 = \mathbf{512}$	**(Length of 9)**
$2 \times 2 \times 2 \times 2 \times 2 \times 2 \times 2 \times 2 \times 2 \times 2 = 1{,}024$	(Length of 10)

The maximum possible length for an integer less than 600 is therefore 9.

18. **(B):** We could solve this problem by computing each answer choice and testing each one to see whether it is divisible by any smaller integer. However, some of the numbers in the answer choices will be very large (for example, 7! is equal to 5,040), so testing to see whether these numbers are prime will be extremely time consuming.

A different approach can be taken: try to find an answer choice which CANNOT be prime based on the properties of divisibility. Earlier in this chapter, we learned the following property of factorials and divisibility: N! is a multiple of all integers from 1 to N. We can apply this concept directly to the answer choices:

(A) 6! − 1: 6! is not prime, but 6! − 1 might be prime, because 6! and 1 do not share any prime factors.
(B) 6! + 21: 6! is not prime, and 6! + 21 CANNOT be prime, because 6! and 21 are both multiples of 3. Therefore, 6! + 21 is divisible by 3.
(C) 6! + 41: 6! is not prime, but 6! + 41 might be prime, because 6! and 41 do not share any prime factors.
(D) 7! − 1: 7! is not prime, but 7! − 1 might be prime, because 7! and 1 do not share any prime factors.
(E) 7! + 11: 7! is not prime, but 7! + 11 might be prime, because 7! and 11 do not share any prime factors.

By the way, because (B) cannot be prime, we can infer that all the other answer choices MUST be prime, without having to actually check them. There **cannot** be more than one correct answer choice.

19. **3:** If x has a remainder of 5 after division by 9 and y has a remainder of 7 after division by 9, then adding the remainders together yields 12. This number is too high, however. The remainder must be non-negative and less than 9. Notice that we can take an additional 9 out of the remainder: $12 − 9 = 3$. Alternatively, we could pick numbers. For example, $x = 14$ and $y = 25$ yields $x + y = 39$, which has a remainder of 3 when divided by 9, because $39 = (4 \times 9) + 3$.

20. **7:** If x has a remainder of 5 after division by 9 and y has a remainder of 7 after division by 9, then subtracting the remainder of x from the remainder of y yields −2. This number is too small, however, since remainders must be non-negative. The remainder must also be less than 9. We have to shift the remainder upwards by adding 9: $−2 + 9 = 7$. Alternatively, we could pick numbers. For example, $x = 23$ and $y = 16$ yields $x − y = 7$, which has a remainder of 7 when divided by 9, because $7 = (0 \times 9) + 7$.

21. **2:** If x has a remainder of 5 after division by 9 and y has a remainder of 7 after division by 9, then subtracting the remainder of y from the remainder of x yields 2. We do not need to adjust this result.

Alternatively, we could pick numbers. For example, $x = 14$ and $y = 25$ yields $y − x = 11$, which has a remainder of 2 when divided by 9, because $11 = (1 \times 9) + 2$.

22. 8: If x has a remainder of 5 after division by 9 and y has a remainder of 7 after division by 9, then multiplying the remainder of x by the remainder of y yields 35. This number is too large—the remainder must be non-negative and must also be less than 9. We have to shift the remainder downward by multiples of 9: $35 - 9 = 26$; $26 - 9 = 17$; and $17 - 9 = 8$. (Or, we could shift 35 down by 27: $35 - (3 \times 9) = 35 - 27 = 8$.)

Alternatively, we could pick numbers. For example, $x = 14$ and $y = 25$ yields $x \cdot y = 350$, which has a remainder of 8 when divided by 9, because $350 = (38 \times 9) + 8$.

23. 0: If x has a remainder of 5 after division by 9 and y has a remainder of 7 after division by 9, then multiplying the remainder of x by 5 and then subtracting the remainder of y yields $(5 \times 5) - 7 = 25 - 7 = 18$. This number is too large—the remainder must be non-negative and must also be less than 9. We have to shift the remainder downward by multiples of 9: $18 - 9 = 9$, and $9 - 9 = 0$. (Or, we could shift 18 down by 18: $18 - (2 \times 9) = 18 - 18 = 0$.) Therefore, $5x - y$ will always be divisible by 9 in this scenario.

Alternatively, we could pick numbers. For example, $x = 14$ and $y = 25$ yields $5x - y = 5(14) - 7 = 70 - 7 = 63$. The number 63 has a remainder of 0 when divided by 9, because $63 = (7 \times 9) + 0$.

24. 30: The remainder must always be smaller than the divisor. In this problem, 5 must be smaller than y. Additionally, y must be an integer, so y must be at least 6. If y is 6, then the smallest possible value of x is 5. (Other values of x that leave a remainder of 5 when divided by 6 would be 11, 17, 23, etc.) If y is chosen to be larger than 6, then the smallest possible value of x is still 5. Thus, we will get the smallest possible value of the product xy by choosing the smallest x together with the smallest y. The smallest possible value of xy is $5 \times 6 = 30$.

25. (A): We can separate the division operation into two components: the integer portion of the result (i.e., the quotient), and the remainder portion of the result:

$$\text{Dividend} \longrightarrow \frac{a}{b} = 3.45 = 3 + 0.45 \longleftarrow \frac{\text{Remainder}}{\text{Divisor}}$$

with Divisor pointing to b, and Quotient pointing to the 3.

The remainder divided by the divisor equals 0.45. Therefore, $R \div b = 0.45$:

$$\frac{R}{b} = 0.45 = \frac{45}{100} = \frac{9}{20}$$

Cross-multiplying leads to:

$$20 \times R = 9 \times b$$

Since R and b must be integers, R must be divisible by 9. The right-hand side of the equation is divisible by 9, so the left-hand side must be divisible by 9. The number 20 does not provide any needed prime factors to help make the left-hand side divisible by 9. Therefore, R must have two 3's in its prime factorization to make the left-hand side divisible by 9. (Incidentally, b must be divisible by 20—the same reasoning applies.)

The only answer choice that is not divisible by 9 is **(A)**.

26. **3, 6, 9, and 18:** There are two ways we can solve this problem effectively. The first way is to pick numbers for y to see which values of y yield a remainder 3 less than y. The second way is to use algebra to determine which values for y are possible.

The first thing to note is that the remainder is $y - 3$. Since the remainder must be non-negative, y must be at least 3.

The second thing to note is that y is at most 18. When $y = 18$, the divisor (18) is 3 larger than 15, and the quotient is zero. As y increases, the remainder will not change. For example, if the divisor is 19, the remainder is still 15 and the quotient is still zero (the divisor is now 4 more than 15). If the divisor is 20, the remainder is still 15 and the quotient is still zero (the divisor is now 5 more than 15). Thus as y increases beyond 18, the difference between y and the remainder will continue to grow, and the remainder will never again be within 3 units of y.

From this point you could pick numbers, dividing 15 by these numbers to check to see whether the remainder is 3 lower than the number you have picked. Only 15 divided by 3, 6, 9, and 18 yield remainders three less than the divisor:

$15 = (5 \times 3) + 0$ Remainder of 0 is 3 less than divisor of 3.
$15 = (2 \times 6) + 3$ Remainder of 3 is 3 less than divisor of 6.
$15 = (1 \times 9) + 6$ Remainder of 6 is 3 less than divisor of 9.
$15 = (0 \times 18) + 15$ Remainder of 15 is 3 less than divisor of 18.

Alternatively, you could take an algebraic approach. The dividend is 15, the divisor is y, the quotient is irrelevant (though it can be represented as x, as a placeholder), and the remainder is $y - 3$:

$$15 = (x \times y) + (y - 3)$$

Now, we can solve for y:

$$18 = xy + y$$
$$18 = y(x + 1)$$

Since x and y must both be integers, this simply tells us that y needs to be a factor of 18. (So does $x + 1$, but the quotient x is irrelevant in this problem). Therefore it appears y could equal 1, 2, 3, 6, 9, or 18.

However, remember that the remainder is $y - 3$ and that remainders must be non-negative. Thus, y cannot equal 1 or 2, because that would make the remainder negative. Therefore, y can equal 3, 6, 9, or 18.

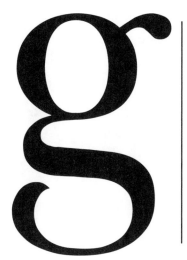

Chapter 11
of
NUMBER PROPERTIES

ODDS & EVENS/
POSITIVES & NEGATIVES/
CONSECUTIVE INTEGERS:
ADVANCED

In This Chapter . . .

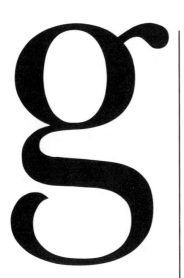

- Special Case of Divisibility (Odds & Evens)
- Representing Evens & Odds Algebraically
- Absolute Value of a Difference
- Disguised Positive & Negative Questions
- Complex Absolute Value Equations
- Consecutive Integers and Divisibility

Special Case of Divisibility (Odds & Evens)

As we have seen, the definition of an even integer is that it is divisible by 2. Therefore, some Odds & Evens problems require analysis using divisibility rules and remainder rules.

If x, y and z are integers and xyz is divisible by 8, is x even?

(1) yz is divisible by 4
(2) x, y, and z are all NOT divisible by 4

xyz

$$2, 2, 2 \\ ... ?$$

The problem stem tells us that xyz is divisible by 8. Therefore, in its prime factorization, xyz has three 2's, and possibly more.

Statement (1) tells us that yz has at least two 2's in it. However, the third 2 could be in x, or it could be in y or z. For example, x could be 2 and yz could be 4, or x could be 1 and yz could be 8. Note that Statement (1) does not preclude the possibility that yz is divisible by 8, 16, etc. INSUFFICIENT.

Statement (2) tells us that x, y, and z do NOT have at least two 2's in them. Since there must be three 2's in xyz, EACH variable must contain one and ONLY one 2 in its prime factorization. Thus, x is even (divisible by 2). SUFFICIENT. The correct answer is **(B)**.

x | y | z

$$2, \not{8}, ... ?$$ $$2, \not{8}, ... ?$$ $$2, \not{8}, ... ?$$

Divisibility by 2 has a special property that divisibility by other numbers does not have. Recall from Chapter 10 that in general when we add or subtract two numbers, neither of which is divisible by x, we cannot tell whether the result will be divisible by x. However, when adding or subtracting two integers, neither of which is divisible by 2, **the result will always be divisible by 2**. (This is an advanced way of saying that the sum or difference of two odd numbers is even.)

Remainder Rules to Remember:
Odd integers are those integers that leave a remainder of 1 after division by 2.
Even integers are those integers that leave a remainder of 0 after division by 2.

If we add two numbers that are odd, the remainder R seems to be $1 + 1 = 2$. However, you cannot have a remainder of 2; the only possible remainders after you divide by 2 are 0 and 1. You then subtract the excess 2 from R, and the remainder R is now 0. Thus, the sum is divisible by 2. Again, we are simply saying that Odd + Odd = Even.

If w, x, y and z are integers and $w + x = y$, is y divisible by z?

(1) w and x each have a remainder of 1 when divided by z
(2) $z = 2$

Manhattan**GMAT**Prep
the new standard

You can solve some Odds & Evens questions can by using principles of Divisibility & Primes.

Statement (1) tells us that w and x are each 1 larger than a multiple of z. If $z = 5$, for example, then w could be 6 and x could be 11. Then y would equal 17, which is NOT divisible by z. However, if $z = 2$, then no matter what numbers we pick for w and x, they must be odd, in which case y is even, or divisible by 2. INSUFFICIENT.

Statement (2) tells us nothing about w, x, or y. INSUFFICIENT.

Statements (1) and (2) combined tell us that w and x are odd, so y must be even and thus divisible by 2. The correct answer is (**C**).

Representing Evens and Odds Algebraically

Even numbers are multiples of 2, so an arbitrary even number can be written as $2n$, where n is any integer. Odd numbers are one more or less than multiples of 2, so an arbitrary odd number can be written as $2n + 1$ or $2n - 1$, where n is an integer.

Using algebra to represent odd and even numbers can be helpful in answering questions in which all that is known about a variable is whether it is odd or even.

> What is the remainder when a is divided by 4 ?
> (1) a is the square of an odd integer.
> (2) a is a multiple of 3.

One way to evaluate Statement (1) is to square a series of odd integers, divide each of the squares by 4, and observe the remainders. However, you can use theory to solve this problem faster.

An arbitrary odd integer can be written $2n + 1$, where n is an integer. Therefore, the square of an arbitrary odd integer can be written as $(2n + 1)^2 = 4n^2 + 4n + 1$. The first two terms of this expression are multiples of 4, which have remainder 0 upon division by 4, so the overall expression must have remainder 1 upon division by 4. Thus, Statement (1) is SUFFICIENT.

Statement (2) can be proven insufficient by picking examples. When 3 is divided by 4, the remainder is 3; when 6 is divided by 4, the remainder is 2. Therefore, statement (2) is INSUFFICIENT. The correct answer is (**A**).

Absolute Value of a Difference

The absolute value $|x - y|$ can be interpreted as **the distance between x and y.** Using this interpretation, you can rephrase $|x - 3| < 4$ as "the distance between x and 3 is less than 4 units," or equivalently, "x is less than 4 units away from 3." This means that $-1 < x < 7$. This concept is also useful in reverse, when you have to write an absolute value equation that shows a particular relationship.

> To perform in a certain youth dance group, girls must be between 4 feet tall (48 inches) and 4 feet 6 inches tall (54 inches), inclusive. If x represents a girl's height, in inches, write an absolute value equation for the heights of girls who are eligible to perform.

Whenever all you know about a variable is whether it is odd or even, consider representing that variable algebraically.

The eligible girls' heights satisfy the double inequality $48 \leq x \leq 54$. To express this inequality in terms of absolute value, we need to find the midpoint, or average, of the range. The average of 48 and 54 is 51 inches.

The eligible girls' heights range from 48 inches, which is 3 **less than** the midpoint of 51 inches, to 54 inches, which is 3 **greater than** 51 inches. Therefore, the distance between x and 51 is at most 3. In other words, $|x - 51| \leq 3$.

On the number line, this looks like:

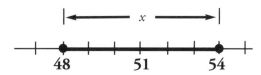

For more on Absolute Value, see the "Complex Absolute Value Equations" section of this chapter and the "Basic Equations Strategy" and "Inequalities" chapters of the Manhattan GMAT *Equations, Inequalities, and VICs* Strategy Guide.

> The absolute value of the difference between x and y is the distance between x and y on the number line.

Disguised Positive & Negative Questions

Some Positives & Negatives questions are disguised as inequalities. This generally occurs whenever a question tells you that a quantity is greater than or less than 0, or asks you whether a quantity is greater than or less than 0.

If $\dfrac{a-b}{c} < 0$, is $a > b$?

(1) $c < 0$
(2) $a + b < 0$

This problem is a disguised Positives & Negatives question, because we are told in several places that a variable expression is greater or less than zero.

The fact that $\dfrac{a-b}{c} < 0$ tells us that $a - b$ and c have DIFFERENT signs. Thus one of the expressions is positive and the other is negative.

Statement (1) tells us that c is negative. Therefore, $a - b$ must be positive:

$a - b > 0$
$a > b$

Statement (1) is SUFFICIENT.

Statement (2) tells us that the sum of a and b is negative. This does not tell us whether a is larger than b. INSUFFICIENT. The correct answer is **(A)**.

Generally speaking, whenever you see inequalities **with zero on either side of the inequality**, you should **consider testing positive/negative cases** to help solve the problem. For more on testing disguised Positive & Negatives problems, see the "Inequalities" chapter of the Manhattan GMAT *Equations, Inequalities, and VICs* Strategy Guide.

Complex Absolute Value Equations

So far we have looked at two basic attributes of absolute value: it is always positive, and it can be interpreted as distance on a number line. Absolute value problems on the GMAT can get more complicated in two primary ways:

(1) The equation or inequality contains **two different variables** in absolute value expressions. These problems, which generally do not have constants in them, are NOT easy to solve algebraically. Rather, a more conceptual approach is preferable.

> With an absolute value equation that contains more than one variable and NO constants, it is usually easiest to test positive/negative numbers to solve the problem.

(2) The equation has more than one absolute value expression but **only one variable** and one or more constants. These equations are *usually* easier to solve with an algebraic approach than a conceptual approach. Problems of this type are discussed in the "Basic Equations Strategy" and "Inequalities" chapters of the Manhattan GMAT *Equations, Inequalities, and VICs* Strategy Guide.

Solving the first type of problem algebraically would require testing several cases, which quickly becomes unmanageable. Hence, try the simpler method of picking and testing numbers, specifically positives, negatives, and zero.

If $|x| - |y| = |x + y|$ and xy does not equal 0, which of the following must be true?

> (A) $x - y > 0$
> (B) $x - y < 0$
> (C) $x + y > 0$
> (D) $xy > 0$
> (E) $xy < 0$

To solve this problem algebraically, we would need to consider many theoretical cases: one for each possible positive/negative/zero combination of the expressions inside the absolute value signs. Since xy does not equal 0, we can eliminate the $x = 0$ and $y = 0$ cases. We can eliminate two more cases upon reflection: x and y cannot be positive while $x + y$ is negative, and x and y cannot be negative while $x + y$ is positive. Still, that leaves many cases to test, and testing these cases would take too much time and be too confusing.

An alternative is that we could pick numbers for x and y and test positive/negative scenarios for them. Note that $|x|$ has to be bigger than or equal to $|y|$, since $|x| - |y|$ is equal to an absolute value and therefore $|x| - |y| \geq 0$ (absolute values cannot be negative):

x	y	$|x| - |y|$	$|x + y|$	**Valid?**
3	2	$|3| - |2| = 1$	$|3 + 2| = 5$	NO
3	−2	$|3| - |-2| = 1$	$|3 + (-2)| = 1$	YES
−3	2	$|-3| - |2| = 1$	$|(-3) + 2| = 1$	YES
−3	−2	$|-3| - |-2| = 1$	$|(-3) + (-2)| = 5$	NO

The cases that work are the those in which the two variables have a DIFFERENT SIGN. The answer is the condition that also obeys this "different sign" criterion: the product of x and y is negative, or **(E) $xy < 0$**.

the new standard

Consecutive Integers and Divisibility

We saw in Part I how we could use prime boxes to track divisibility for consecutive integers. Problems involving these concepts can become very difficult. Consider this example:

If $x^3 - x = p$, and x is odd, is p divisible by 24?

If we factor x out of the expression $x^3 - x$, we get $x(x^2 - 1)$. If we further factor this expression, we get $x(x + 1)(x - 1)$. If we rearrange these terms, we can see that this is a product of consecutive integers:

$$p = (x - 1)x(x + 1)$$

If x is odd, then $(x - 1)$ and $(x + 1)$ must be even. Thus, p is divisible by at least 4. Furthermore, $(x - 1)$ and $(x + 1)$ are consecutive multiples of 2. So either $(x - 1)$ or $(x + 1)$ must have another 2 and be divisible by 4. Therefore, p is divisible by 8.

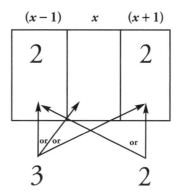

In addition, one of the numbers—$(x - 1)$, x, or $(x + 1)$—is divisible by 3, because in any set of 3 consecutive integers,
one of the integers will be a multiple of 3. We can therefore conclude that if x is odd, p will be divisible by at least $2 \times 2 \times 2 \times 3 = 24$.

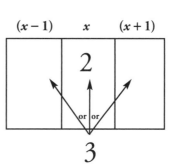

Note that if we were told that x is even, we would have the product of two odd integers and one even integer. One even number in the product would guarantee that the product would be divisible by 2. The product would also be divisible by 3, as before. However, we would not know anything more about the prime factors of the product. Therefore, unless we also knew that x itself were divisible by 8, 24 would not necessarily be a factor of p.

Be on the lookout for tough problems involving the NECESSARY prime factors of the product of a given number of consecutive integers.

Problem Set (Advanced)

1. If p, q, and r are integers, is $pq + r$ even?

    (1) $p + r$ is even.
    (2) $q + r$ is odd.

2. If $k = 2n - 1$, where n is an integer, what is the remainder of $\dfrac{k^2}{8}$?

    (A) 1
    (B) 3
    (C) 5
    (D) 7
    (E) Cannot be determined from the information given.

3. If x, y, and z are prime numbers and $x < y < z$, what is the value of x?

    (1) xy is even.
    (2) xz is even.

4. If c and d are integers, is $c - 3d$ even?

    (1) c and d are odd.
    (2) $c - 2d$ is odd.

5. For each of the following, what are the possible remainders upon division by 4?

    (A) The product of two consecutive even integers
    (B) The square of an odd integer
    (C) The square of an even integer
    (D) The product of two consecutive odd integers
    (E) The product of two consecutive integers

6. Classify each of the following as ALWAYS an integer, SOMETIMES an integer, or NEVER an integer:

    (A) An even number divided by a smaller even number
    (B) An even number divided by a smaller odd number
    (C) An odd number divided by a smaller even number
    (D) An odd number divided by a smaller odd number

7. Which of the following inequalities is equivalent to the shaded part of the number line shown to the right?

    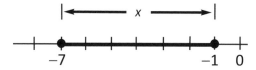

    (A) $|x| \geq -7$ (B) $|x - 4| \geq 3$ (C) $|x + 4| \leq 3$
    (D) $|x| \leq -1$ (E) $|x + 3| \leq 4$

8.   Is $pqr > 0$?

      (1) $pq > 0$

      (2) $\dfrac{q}{r} < 0$

9.   If $x \neq 0$, is $-\dfrac{x}{|x|} = 1$?

      (1) $-x|x| > 0$
      (2) $x^2 = 9$

10.   Which values of x are solutions to the inequality $|x + 1| + |x - 1| \leq 2$? (Hint: try a conceptual approach. Your answer will be an inequality as well.)

11.   A machinist's salary at a factory increases by $2,000 at the end of each full year the machinist works. If the machinist's salary for the fifth year is $39,000, what is the machinist's average annual salary for his first 21 years at the factory?

12.   Is the average of n consecutive integers equal to 1?

      (1) n is even.
      (2) If S is the sum of the n consecutive integers, then $0 < S < n$.

13.   The product $7 \times 6 \times 5 \times 4 \times 3$ is divisible by all of the following EXCEPT:

      (A) 120   (B) 240   (C) 360   (D) 840   (E) 1260

14.   If S is a set of consecutive integers, what is the sum of the elements in S?

      (1) The largest element in S is 55.
      (2) There are 11 elements in S.

1. **(E):** Statement (1) tells us that $p + r$ is even. Therefore both p and r are even, or both p and r are odd. For each of those scenarios, q could be odd or even. We need to set up a table to analyze all of these possibilities:

Scenario	p	q	r	$pq + r$
1	ODD	ODD	ODD	$O \times O + O = E$
2	ODD	EVEN	ODD	$O \times E + O = O$
3	EVEN	ODD	EVEN	$E \times O + O = O$
4	EVEN	EVEN	EVEN	$O \times E + E = E$

Since $pq + r$ could be odd or even, Statement (1) is INSUFFICIENT.

Similarly, we can evaluate Statement (2) with a scenario table. The variables q and r must either both be odd or both be even, and p can be odd or even:

Scenario	p	q	r	$pq + r$
5	ODD	EVEN	ODD	$O \times E + O = O$
6	EVEN	EVEN	ODD	$E \times E + O = O$
7	ODD	ODD	EVEN	$O \times O + E = O$
8	EVEN	ODD	EVEN	$E \times O + E = E$

Thus Statement (2) is INSUFFICIENT.

Notice that Scenarios 2 and 5 are identical, as are Scenarios 3 and 8. Therefore both sets of scenarios meet the criteria laid forth in Statements (1) and (2), but they yield opposite answers to the question:

Scenario	p	q	r	$pq + r$
2 & 5	ODD	EVEN	ODD	$O \times E + O = O$
3 & 8	EVEN	ODD	EVEN	$E \times O + E = E$

Since both scenarios are possible, Statements (1) and (2) combined are INSUFFICIENT. The correct answer is (E).

2. **(A) 1:** Since $k = 2n - 1$, we can represent k^2 as:

$$k^2 = (2n-1)^2 = 4n^2 - 4n + 1$$

We can factor this expression as follows:

$$k = 4n(n - 1) + 1$$

If n is even, then $n - 1$ is odd, while if n is odd, then $n - 1$ is even. Therefore no matter what integer n is, k will equal 4 × even × odd, plus 1. In other words, k will equal a multiple of 8, plus 1. Therefore, the remainder of $\dfrac{k^2}{8}$ is 1.

3. **(D):** If xy is even, then x is even or y is even. Since $x < y$, x must equal 2, because 2 is the smallest and only even prime number. Statement (1) is SUFFICIENT.

Similarly, If xz is even, then x is even or z is even. Since $x < z$, x must equal 2, because 2 is the smallest and only even prime number. Statement (2) is SUFFICIENT.

4. **(A):** If both c and d are odd, then $c - 3d$ equals O $- (3 \times$ O$) =$ O $-$ O $=$ E. Statement (1) is SUFFICIENT.

If $c - 2d$ is odd, then c must be odd, because $2d$ will always be even. However, this tells us nothing about d. Statement (2) is INSUFFICIENT.

5. **(A): 0, (B): 1, (C): 0, (D): 3, (E): 0 or 2**
(A) Each of the two even integers is divisible by 2. Therefore, the product is divisible by 2 twice, making it divisible by 4. Therefore, since the product is evenly divisible by 4, it must leave a remainder of 0 upon division by 4. Alternatively, write an algebraic expression for consecutive even integers, $2n$ and $2n + 2$, and multiply them, giving $2n(2n + 2) = 4n^2 + 4n$. Both terms of this expression are divisible by 4, making the whole expression divisible by 4. Therefore, the remainder upon division by 4 is zero.

(B) A generic expression for an odd integer is $2n + 1$; squaring gives $(2n + 1)^2 = 4n^2 + 4n + 1$. Since the first two terms are multiples of 4, the remainder upon division by 4 is $0 + 0 + 1 = 1$. Alternatively, we know that Odd $\div$ 4 leaves R1 or R3. Odd$^2 = $ (R1)(R1) $=$ R1 OR (R3)(R3) $=$ R9 $=$ R1 (taking out two 4's).

(C) A generic expression for an even integer is $2n$; squaring gives $(2n)^2 = 4n^2$. Since this is a multiple of 4, the remainder upon division by 4 is 0.

(D) A generic expression for consecutive odd integers is $2n + 1$ and $2n + 3$; multiplication yields $(2n + 1)(2n + 3) = 4n^2 + 8n + 3$. Since the first two terms are multiples of 4, the remainder upon division by 4 is $0 + 0 + 3 = 3$. Alternatively, we know that Odd $\div$ 4 leaves R1 or R3. The product of (Odd)(Odd + 2) $=$ (R1)(R3) $=$ R9 $=$ R1 (taking out two 4's).

(E) Examine the first three products of consecutive integers: $1 \times 2 = 2$, $2 \times 3 = 6$, $3 \times 4 = 12$. The first two products leave a remainder of 2 upon division by 4, but the last leaves a remainder of 0. Therefore, there is not a unique remainder, and the remainder would be 0 or 2 (Note that the product will always be even, so the remainder cannot be 1 or 3).

6. **(A): SOMETIMES,** depending on whether the smaller integer contains any prime factors that are not also part of the larger integer. For instance, $\dfrac{8}{4}$ is an integer, but $\dfrac{8}{6}$ is not (because the prime factorization of 6 contains 3, a factor not present in the prime factorization of 8).

(B): SOMETIMES, depending on whether the smaller integer contains any prime factors that are not also part of the larger integer. For instance, $\dfrac{6}{3}$ is an integer, but $\dfrac{6}{5}$ is not (because the prime factorization of 5 is 5, a factor not present in the prime factorization of 6).

(C): NEVER. All even numbers, no matter how small, contain at least one 2 in their prime factorization. However, no odd number has a 2 in its prime factorization. Therefore, this quotient can never be an integer, because at least one "2" in the denominator will not cancel.

(D): SOMETIMES, depending on whether the smaller integer contains any prime factors that are not also part of the larger integer. For instance, $\dfrac{9}{3}$ is an integer, but $\dfrac{9}{5}$ is not (because the prime factorization of 5 is 5, a factor not present in the prime factorization of 9).

7. **(C)** $|x + 4| \leq 3$: The first step for this problem is to find the midpoint of the region in the graph. The midpoint is the average of the endpoints (−1 and −7), which is −4. Next, notice that the maximum possible distance that x can be away from −4 is 3 units (−1 is 3 greater than −4, and −7 is 3 less than −4). Therefore, $x - (-4)$, or $x + 4$, cannot be more than 3 or less than −3. Thus, $|x + 4| \leq 3$.

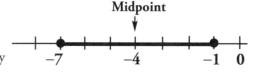

8. **(E):** Statement (1) tells us that p and q have the same sign. This tells us nothing about r, so Statement (1) is INSUFFICIENT. Statement (2) tells us that q and r have opposite signs. This tells us nothing about p, so Statement (2) is INSUFFICIENT. Combined, we know that p and q have the same sign, and r has the opposite sign. If p and q are positive, r is negative and pqr is negative. If p and q are negative, r is positive and pqr is positive. INSUFFICIENT. The correct answer is (E).

9. **(A):** If $-\dfrac{x}{|x|} = 1$, it must be true that $-x = |x|$. This will only be true when x is negative. Statement (1) tells us that $-x|x|$ is positive. Since $|x|$ cannot be negative, this implies that $-x$ is positive, so x is negative. SUFFICIENT. Statement (2) tells us that $|x| = 3$, so $x = 3$ or −3. This does not tells us whether x is negative. INSUFFICIENT. The correct answer is (A).

10. **$-1 \leq x \leq 1$:** Even though this problem only contains one variable, it is extremely difficult to solve with algebra. However, you can interpret the absolute values as distance expressions: The distance of x from −1, plus the distance of x from 1, is smaller than or equal to 2.

Draw a number line, separating it into three regions according to the points −1 and 1:

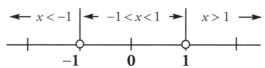

No point in the left-hand region can satisfy the inequality, because if x is less than −1, then the distance between x and 1 is larger than 2. Similarly, if x is larger than 1, then its distance from −1 is larger than 2. For any point in the middle region, though—including −1 and 1 themselves—the distances from −1 to x and from x to 1 add up to exactly 2. If, for example, $x = 0.2$, then the distance to −1 is 1.2, and the distance to 1 is 0.8. We see that $1.2 + 0.8 = 2$. You can demonstrate that this will be true for any value of x that satisfies $-1 \leq x \leq 1$.

11. **$51,000:** The annual salaries of the machinist are an evenly spaced set, because each year the salary increases by the same amount. From the properties of evenly spaced sets, we know that the number we are seeking is both the median and the mean of the 21-year salary scale. It is also the average of the first and last years' salaries:

$$\text{Average Salary} = \frac{(\text{First year's salary}) + (\text{Last year's salary})}{2}$$

To find the salaries for the first and twenty-first years, use the fact that the salaries increase by constant increments of $2,000 per year.

The 1st year is four years before the fifth year, so the 1st year salary is $39,000 − 4(2,000) = $31,000. The 21st year is sixteen years after the fifth year, so the 21st year salary is $39,000 + 16(2,000) = $71,000.

Therefore, the average salary for all 21 years is $\dfrac{(\$31,000 + \$71,000)}{2} = \$51,000$.

12. **(D):** Statement (1) states that there is an even number of consecutive integers. This statement tells us nothing about the actual values of the integers, but the average of an even number of consecutive integers will never be an integer. Therefore, the average of the n consecutive integers cannot equal 1. SUFFICIENT.

Statement (2) tells us that the sum of the n consecutive integers is positive, but smaller than n. Perhaps the most straightforward way to interpret this statement is to express it in terms of the average of the n numbers, rather than the sum. Average = Sum ÷ Number, so we can reinterpret the statement by dividing the compound inequality by n:

$$0 < S < n \qquad\qquad \frac{0}{n} < \frac{S}{n} < \frac{n}{n} \qquad\qquad 0 < \frac{S}{n} < 1$$

This tells us that the average integer in set S is larger than 0 but less than 1. Therefore, the average number in the set does NOT equal 1. SUFFICIENT. The correct answer is (D).

As a footnote, this situation can happen ONLY when there is an even number of integers, and when the "middle numbers" in the set are 0 and 1. For example, the set of consecutive integers {0, 1} has a median number of 0.5. Similarly, the set of consecutive integers {−3, −2, −1, 0, 1, 2, 3, 4} has a median number of 0.5.

13. **(B) 240:** First, determine the prime factorization of the product:

$$7 \times 6 \times 5 \times 4 \times 3 = 7 \times (3 \times 2) \times 5 \times (2 \times 2) \times 3 = 2^3 \times 3^2 \times 5 \times 7.$$

Next, write the prime factorization of each answer choice and determine which choice has a prime factor that is NOT in the prime factorization of the product above. Note that you can re-use a lot of your work, because the answer choices share many common prime factors.

(A): $120 = 10 \times 12 = 2^3 \times 3 \times 5$. All of these primes are in the factorization of $7 \times 6 \times 5 \times 4 \times 3$.

(B): $240 = 10 \times 24 = 2^4 \times 3 \times 5$. There is an extra 2 in this factorization that is NOT part of the factorization of $7 \times 6 \times 5 \times 4 \times 3$. Therefore, the product is not divisible by 240.

(C): $360 = 10 \times 36 = 2^3 \times 3^2 \times 5$. All of these primes are in the factorization of $7 \times 6 \times 5 \times 4 \times 3$.

(D): $840 = 10 \times 12 \times 7 = 2^3 \times 3 \times 5 \times 7$. All of these primes are in the factorization of $7 \times 6 \times 5 \times 4 \times 3$.

(E): $1260 = 10 \times 18 \times 7 = 2^2 \times 3^2 \times 5 \times 7$. All of these primes are in the factorization of $7 \times 6 \times 5 \times 4 \times 3$.

An alternative method is to recognize that $120 = 5!$, which is a factor of the product of any 5 consecutive integers. Thus, answer choice (A) can be eliminated. Going further, we can rearrange $7 \times 6 \times 5 \times 4 \times 3$ as the product $7 \times 3 \times 2 \times 5 \times 4 \times 3$, which in turn can be rewritten as $7 \times 3 \times 5!$. Since $240 = 2 \times 5!$, we can now observe that $(7 \times 3 \times 5!) \div (2 \times 5!) = 21 \div 2$, which is not an integer. This tells us that (B) is the right answer.

14. **(C):** Statement (1) tells us that the largest (last) element in S is 55. However, we do not know how many elements are in S, or what the smallest (first) number in S is, so we cannot determine the average. For example, if the smallest number is 53, then the average is $(53 + 55) \div 2 = 54$. If the smallest number is 11, then the average is $(11 + 55) \div 2 = 33$. INSUFFICIENT.

Statement (2) tells us that there are 11 elements in the set. However, we know nothing about the size of the numbers in S. For example, if S is the set of integers from 1 to 11, the average is $(1 + 11) \div 2 = 6$. If S is the set of integers from 35 to 45, the average is $(35 + 45) \div 2 = 40$. INSUFFICIENT.

Combining Statements (1) and (2), we know that 55 is the largest element in S and there are 11 elements in S. Using the formula for the number of terms in a set of consecutive integers, we can find the smallest number in the set:

$$\text{Number of terms} = (\text{Last} - \text{First}) + 1$$
$$11 = (55 - \text{First}) + 1$$
$$\text{First} = 55 + 1 - 11 = 45$$

Therefore, Set S is the set of consecutive integers from 45 to 55. The average of the elements in S is $(45 + 55) \div 2 = 50$, and there are 11 elements. The sum of the elements is $50(11) = 550$. SUFFICIENT.

The correct answer is **(C)**. Note that we did not need to compute this sum, because we knew three required pieces of information: (a) the last number in the series, which is 55; (b) the increment, which is 1; and (c) the number of terms, which is 11. As mentioned in the text, these three pieces of information fully define ANY evenly spaced set.

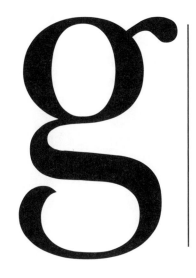

Chapter 12
of
NUMBER PROPERTIES

EXPONENTS & ROOTS: ADVANCED

In This Chapter . . .

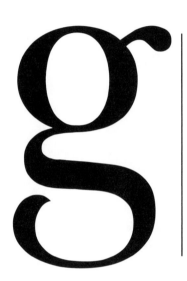

- Simplifying Exponential Expressions
- Factoring and Distributing Exponents
- Simplifying Roots with Prime Factorization
- Adding and Subtracting Roots
- Using Conjugates to Rationalize Denominators

Simplifying Exponential Expressions

As we saw in Part I, **whenever two or more terms with exponents are added or subtracted, consider factoring the terms**. There may be common factors across the terms that can be factored out.

Simplify the following expression: $\dfrac{\left(7^5+7^7\right)4^5}{8^3 \cdot 25}$

This type of expression can be factored by applying rules of exponents using a **4-step process**. Use this process whenever a problem contains multiple exponential terms that need to be combined—especially if some of the terms share common prime factors:

4-Step Process

1. Simplify or factor any additive or subtractive terms

2. Break every non-prime base down into prime factors

3. Distribute the exponents to every prime factor

4. Combine the exponents for each prime factor and simplify

$$\frac{\left(7^5+7^7\right)4^5}{8^3 \cdot 25}=\frac{7^5\left(1+7^2\right)4^5}{8^3 \cdot 25}=\frac{7^5\left(50\right)4^5}{8^3 \cdot 25}$$

$$\frac{7^5\left(50\right)4^5}{8^3 \cdot 25}=\frac{7^5 \times (5 \cdot 5 \cdot 2) \times (2 \cdot 2)^5}{(2 \cdot 2 \cdot 2)^3 (5 \cdot 5)}$$

$$\frac{7^5 \times (5 \cdot 5 \cdot 2) \times (2 \cdot 2)^5}{(2 \cdot 2 \cdot 2)^3 (5 \cdot 5)}=\frac{7^5 \times 5^1 \times 5^1 \times 2^1 \times 2^5 \times 2^5}{2^3 \times 2^3 \times 2^3 \times 5^1 \times 5^1}$$

$$\frac{7^5 \times 5^1 \times 5^1 \times 2^1 \times 2^5 \times 2^5}{2^3 \times 2^3 \times 2^3 \times 5^1 \times 5^1}=\frac{7^5 \times 5^{(1+1)} \times 2^{(1+5+5)}}{2^{(3+3+3)} \times 5^{(1+1)}}=$$

$$\frac{7^5 \times 5^2 \times 2^{11}}{2^9 \times 5^2}=7^5 \times 5^{(2-2)} \times 2^{(11-9)}=7^5 \cdot 2^2$$

> The 4-step process can help you simplify even the most difficult exponential expressions.

This process may not be the fastest way to combine exponential expressions such as this one (for example, the "5" terms in the numerator and denominator could have been eliminated earlier on). However, if you apply the prime factorizations and rules of exponents correctly, these steps will always lead you to the right answer.

Factoring and Distributing of Exponents

As discussed earlier, GMAT problems often contain exponential expressions that can be factored or distributed. Distributing a factored expression or factoring a distributed expression can often help the solution process. A general rule of thumb is that **when you encounter any exponential expression in which two or more terms include something common in the base, you should consider factoring**. Similarly, **when an expression is given in factored form, consider distributing it**. It is especially important to note that you should feel comfortable going both ways: from distributed form to factored form, and vice versa

Below are some advanced examples of factored and distributed exponential expressions that are equivalent. For more on Factoring and Distributing, please see the "Basic Equations" chapter of Manhattan GMAT's *Equations, Inequalities, and VICs* strategy guide.

DISTRIBUTED FORM	FACTORED FORM
$x^2 - x$	$x(x-1)$
$x^4 - x^2$	$x^2(x^2-1) = x^2(x+1)(x-1)$
$7^5 - 7^3$	$7^3(7^2-1) = 48 \cdot 7^3$
$5^8 + 5^9 + 5^{10}$	$5^8(1+5+5^2) = 31 \cdot 5^8$
$z^3 - z$	$z(z^2-1) = z(z+1)(z-1)$
$10^{(b+1)}$	$10(10^b)$
$10^{(b-1)}$	$\dfrac{(10^b)}{10}$
$3^5 + 3^5 + 3^5$	$3(3^5) = 3^6$
$a^b - a^{b-1}$	$a^b(1-a^{-1}) = a^{b-1}(a-1)$
$pq + pr + qs + rs$	$p(q+r) + s(q+r) =$ $(p+s)(q+r)$

Look for different ways to factor or distribute exponential expressions.

Simplifying Roots with Prime Factorization

Because the GMAT is multiple-choice—and because you are not allowed to use a calculator—you should recognize different forms of the same expression.

To simplify a root, follow this procedure:
  (1) Factor the number under the radical sign into primes.
  (2) Pull out any pair of matching primes from under the radical sign, and place one of those primes outside the root. (When you do this step, you are using the property that defines square roots: $\sqrt{x \cdot x} = x$, where x is any positive number.)
  (3) Consolidate the expression.

Consider this example:

Simplify $\sqrt{180}$.

First, factor 180 into primes, yielding $\sqrt{3 \cdot 3 \cdot 2 \cdot 2 \cdot 5}$. Next, remove each pair of primes and replace it with a single prime for that pair OUTSIDE of the radical:

$\sqrt{3 \cdot 3 \cdot 2 \cdot 2 \cdot 5} = (3 \cdot 2) \cdot \sqrt{5}$. Finally, consolidate the 3 and 2, yielding $6\sqrt{5}$.

> Non-prime numbers under the radical can often be broken down into primes and simplified; sometimes this can lead to terms that can be added or subtracted.

Adding and Subtracting Roots

Roots act like variables in addition and subtraction: you can only combine them if they are "like terms" or similar terms. In other words, you cannot combine $\sqrt{3}$ and $\sqrt{5}$ in the expression $\sqrt{3} + \sqrt{5}$. The only root expressions you can combine in sums or differences are expressions that, once simplified, have the same number under the radical sign.

Therefore, you must simplify roots before you add or subtract them to see whether the final number under the radical is the same. Sometime roots that do not appear at first to be similar can in fact be combined.

Simplify $\sqrt{80} - \sqrt{45}$.

First, factor each number under the radical into primes. Then, simplify by removing the pairs of primes and placing one number from each pair outside the radical, and consolidate:

$$\sqrt{80} - \sqrt{45} = \sqrt{2 \cdot 2 \cdot 2 \cdot 2 \cdot 5} - \sqrt{3 \cdot 3 \cdot 5} = (2 \cdot 2)\sqrt{5} - 3\sqrt{5} = 4\sqrt{5} - 3\sqrt{5}$$

Because the remaining number under the radical sign is identical in both terms, we can combine these terms when we subtract:

$$4\sqrt{5} - 3\sqrt{5} = \sqrt{5}$$

This result is probably unexpected. This is why you must always simplify roots.

Using Conjugates to Rationalize Denominators

Some GMAT problems involve fractions that contain square roots in the denominator. When the denominator is a square root alone, it is easy to simplify the fraction by simply multiplying the numerator and denominator by the square root:

Simplify $\dfrac{4}{\sqrt{2}}$.

By multiplying the numerator and denominator by the square root, we can remove the root from the denominator entirely:

$$\frac{4}{\sqrt{2}} \times \left(\frac{\sqrt{2}}{\sqrt{2}}\right) = \frac{4\sqrt{2}}{2} = 2\sqrt{2}$$

However, simplifying a denominator that contains the sum or difference of a square root AND another term is more difficult:

Simplify $\dfrac{4}{3-\sqrt{2}}$.

To simplify this type of problem, we need to use **the conjugate** of the denominator. The conjugate for any square root expression involving addition or subtraction is defined as follows:

For $a + \sqrt{b}$, the conjugate is given by $a - \sqrt{b}$.

For $a - \sqrt{b}$, the conjugate is given by $a + \sqrt{b}$.

In other words, simply change the sign of the square root term to find the conjugate. By multiplying the numerator and denominator by the conjugate, we eliminate the square root from the denominator:

$$\frac{4}{3-\sqrt{2}}\left(\frac{3+\sqrt{2}}{3+\sqrt{2}}\right) = \frac{4(3+\sqrt{2})}{(3-\sqrt{2})(3+\sqrt{2})} = \frac{12+4\sqrt{2}}{9+3\sqrt{2}-3\sqrt{2}-2} = \frac{12+4\sqrt{2}}{7}$$

Use the conjugate to rationalize the denominator of any fraction with a square root PLUS OR MINUS another term.

Problem Set (Advanced)

1. If $x^3 = x^{15}$, and $x > 0$, what is x?

2. If $a^2 = 64$ and $b^4 = 1$, what are all the possible values of ab?

3. Simplify: $\dfrac{m^8 p^7 r^{12}}{m^3 r^9 p} \times p^2 r^3 m^4$

4. Which of the follow expressions has the largest value?

    (A) $(3^4)^{13}$ (B) $\left[(3^{30})^{12} \right]^{1/10}$ (C) $3^{30} + 3^{30} + 3^{30}$ (D) $4(3^{51})$ (E) $\left(3^{100} \right)^{1/2}$

5. (a) What is the greatest common factor of the terms in the expression
    $(4^{15} + 4^{16} + 4^{17} + 4^{18})$?

    (b) Factor out the greatest common factor ascertained in part (a), and simplify the
    resulting expression to an integer multiple of that common factor.

6. Simplify: $(4^y + 4^y + 4^y + 4^y)(3^y + 3^y + 3^y)$

7. If $4^a + 4^{a+1} = 4^{a+2} - 176$, what is the value of a?

8. If $a = 5^{20} - 5^{19} + 5^{18}$, what is the length of a? (The length of an integer is the number of
    prime numbers, not necessarily distinct, in the prime factorization of the integer.)

9. If m and n are positive integers and $(2^{18})(5^m) = (20^n)$, what is the value of m?

10. If x, y, and z are integers, is x even?

    (1) $10^x = (4^y)(5^z)$
    (2) $3^{x+5} = 27^{y+1}$

11. Which of the following is equivalent to $\left(\dfrac{1}{3} \right)^{-4} \left(\dfrac{1}{9} \right)^{-3} \left(\dfrac{1}{27} \right)^{-2}$?

    (A) $\left(\dfrac{1}{3} \right)^{-8}$ (B) $\left(\dfrac{1}{3} \right)^{-9}$ (C) $\left(\dfrac{1}{3} \right)^{-16}$ (D) $\left(\dfrac{1}{3} \right)^{-18}$ (E) $\left(\dfrac{1}{3} \right)^{-144}$

For #12–14, write the expression in factored form (if distributed) and in distributed form (if factored):

12. $z^4 - z^2$

13. $b^a - b^{a+1}$

14. $(a+b)(r+s)$

For #15–25, either solve or simplify, using the properties of roots:

15. $25^{-\frac{1}{2}}$

16.   Estimate $4\sqrt{3}$ to the nearest tenth.

17. $\sqrt{150} - \sqrt{50}$

18. $\sqrt{150} - \sqrt{96}$

19. $\sqrt{x^4}$

20. $\sqrt{20(4) - 5(7)}$

21. $\sqrt{2a + 7a}$, assuming a is positive.

22. $\sqrt[3]{\sqrt[4]{5}}$

23. $\dfrac{\sqrt[4]{64}}{\sqrt[4]{4}}$

24. $\dfrac{1}{\sqrt{x} + \sqrt{x+1}}$, assuming $x > 0$.

25. $\dfrac{4}{8 + 3\sqrt{7}}$

26.   Which of the following is equal to $\dfrac{6 + \sqrt{5}}{2 - \sqrt{5}}$?

     (A) 17   (B) −17   (C) $17 + 8\sqrt{5}$ (D) $-17 - 8\sqrt{5}$ (E) $12 + 12\sqrt{5}$

1. **1:** If $x^3 = x^{15}$, x could be -1, 0, or 1. Given the additional fact that $x > 0$, x can only be 1.

2. **8 and -8:** If $a^2 = 64$, a can be either 8 or -8. If $b^4 = 1$, b can be either 1 or -1. Therefore, the product ab can be equal to either 8 or -8.

3. $\mathbf{m^9 p^8 r^6}$: $\dfrac{m^8 p^7 r^{12}}{m^3 r^9 p} \times p^2 r^3 m^4 = \dfrac{m^{12} p^9 r^{15}}{m^3 r^9 p} = m^{(12-3)} p^{(9-1)} r^{(15-9)} = m^9 p^8 r^6$

4. **(D) $4(3^{51})$:** Use the rules of exponents to simplify each expression:

   (A) $(3^4)^{13} = 3^{52}$

   (B) $\left[(3^{30})^{12}\right]^{1/10} = \left(3^{360}\right)^{1/10} = 3^{360/10} = 3^{36}$

   (C) $3^{30} + 3^{30} + 3^{30} = 3(3^{30}) = 3^{31}$

   (D) $4(3^{51})$ cannot be simplified further.

   (E) $\left(3^{100}\right)^{1/2} = 3^{100/2} = 3^{50}$

Answer choice (A) is clearly larger than (B), (C), and (E). We must now compare $4(3^{51})$ to 3^{52}. To make them most easily comparable, factor one 3 out of 3^{52}: $3^{52} = 3(3^{51})$. $4(3^{51})$ is greater than $3(3^{51})$, so (D) is the correct answer.

5. **(a) 4^{15}:** Just as the greatest common factor of the terms in $x^{15} + x^{16} + x^{17} + x^{18}$ would be x^{15}, the greatest common factor of the terms in $4^{15} + 4^{16} + 4^{17} + 4^{18}$ is 4^{15}.

   (b) $85(4^{15})$: Factor 4^{15} out of the expression the same way you would factor x^{15} out of the expression $x^{15} + x^{16} + x^{17} + x^{18}$:

$$4^{15} + 4^{16} + 4^{17} + 4^{18} = 4^{15}(4^0 + 4^1 + 4^2 + 4^3) = 4^{15}(1 + 4 + 16 + 64) = 85(4^{15})$$

6. **$(12)^{y+1}$:** $(4^y + 4^y + 4^y + 4^y)(3^y + 3^y + 3^y) = (4 \cdot 4^y)(3 \cdot 3^y) = (4^{y+1})(3^{y+1}) = (4 \cdot 3)^{y+1} = (12)^{y+1}$

7. **2:** The key to this problem is to express all of the exponential terms in terms of the greatest common factor of the terms: 4^a. Using the addition rule (or the corresponding numerical examples), we get:

   $$\begin{array}{ll}
   4^a + 4^{a+1} = 4^{a+2} - 176 & 176 = 4^a \cdot (16 - 1 - 4) \\
   176 = 4^{a+2} - 4^a - 4^{a+1} & 176 = 4^a \cdot (11) \\
   176 = 4^a \cdot (4^2) - 4^a - 4^a \cdot (4^1) & 4^a = 176 \div 11 = 16 \\
   176 = 4^a \cdot (4^2 - 4^0 - 4^1) & a = 2
   \end{array}$$

8. **20:** The first step is to factor the greatest common factor (5^{18}) out of each of the terms:

   $$\begin{array}{ll}
   a = 5^{20} - 5^{19} + 5^{18} & a = 5^{18}(21) \\
   a = 5^{18}(5^2 - 5^1 + 5^0) & a = 5^{18} \cdot 3 \cdot 7 \\
   a = 5^{18}(25 - 5 + 1) &
   \end{array}$$

a contains eighteen 5's, one 3, and one 7. Thus, a has 20 total primes, so the length of a is 20.

9. **9:** With exponential equations such as this one, the key is to recognize that as long as the exponents are all integers, each side of the equation must have the same number of each type of prime factor. Break down each base into prime factors and set the exponents equal to each other:

$$(2^{18})(5^m) = (20^n)$$
$$2^{18} \cdot 5^m = (2 \cdot 2 \cdot 5)^n$$
$$2^{18} \cdot 5^m = 2^{2n} \cdot 5^n$$
$$18 = 2n; \; m = n$$
$$n = 9; \; m = n = 9$$

⟵

Because m and n have to be integers, there must be the **same number of 2's** on either side of the equation, and there must be the **same number of 5's** on either side of the equation. Thus $18 = 2n$ and $m = n$.

10. **(A):** Statement (1) tells us that $10^x = (4^y)(5^z)$. We can break the bases down into prime factors: $(2 \cdot 5)^x = (2 \cdot 2)^y \cdot 5^z$, so $2^x \cdot 5^x = 2^{2y} \cdot 5^z$. This tells us that $x = 2y$ and $x = z$. (We need the same numbers of 2's and the same number of 5's on either side of the equation.) SUFFICIENT: y is an integer, so x must be even, because $x = 2y$.

Statement (2) tells us that $3^{x+5} = 27^{y+1}$. We can again break the bases down into prime factors: $3^{x+5} = (3 \cdot 3 \cdot 3)^{y+1}$, so $3^{x+5} = 3^{3y+3}$. This tells us that $x + 5 = 3y + 3$, so $x + 2 = 3y$. (Again, we need the same number of 3's on either side of the equation.) INSUFFICIENT: y is an integer, so x must be 2 larger than a multiple of 3, but that does not tell us whether x is even. If $y = 1$, then $x = 5$ (odd), but if $y = 2$, then $x = 8$ (even).

The correct answer is **(A):** Statement (1) ALONE is sufficient.

11. **(C)** $\left(\dfrac{1}{3}\right)^{-16}$: Once again, we should break each base down into its prime factors first. Then, we apply the negative exponent by taking the reciprocal of each term, and making the exponent positive:

$$\left(\frac{1}{3}\right)^{-4}\left(\frac{1}{9}\right)^{-3}\left(\frac{1}{27}\right)^{-2} = \left(\frac{1}{3}\right)^{-4}\left(\frac{1}{3^2}\right)^{-3}\left(\frac{1}{3^3}\right)^{-2} = 3^4 \times (3^2)^3 \times (3^3)^2 = 3^4 \times 3^6 \times 3^6 = 3^{4+6+6} = 3^{16}$$

Because all of the answer choices have negative exponents, we can perform the same transformation on them—simply take the reciprocal of each and change the exponent to a positive:

(A) $\left(\dfrac{1}{3}\right)^{-8} = 3^8$ (D) $\left(\dfrac{1}{3}\right)^{-18} = 3^{18}$

(B) $\left(\dfrac{1}{3}\right)^{-9} = 3^9$ (E) $\left(\dfrac{1}{3}\right)^{-144} = 3^{144}$

(C) $\left(\dfrac{1}{3}\right)^{-16} = \mathbf{3^{16}}$

12. $z^4 - z^2 = z^2(z^2 - 1) = z^2(z+1)(z-1)$

13. $b^a - b^{a+1} = b^a(1-b)$

14. $(a+b)(r+s) = ar + as + br + bs$

15. $\dfrac{1}{5}$: $25^{-\frac{1}{2}} = \dfrac{1}{25^{\frac{1}{2}}} = \dfrac{1}{\sqrt{25}} = \dfrac{1}{5}$

16. **6.9:** $4\sqrt{3}$ can be combined into one radical: $\sqrt{4} \times \sqrt{4} \times \sqrt{3} = \sqrt{4 \times 4 \times 3} = \sqrt{48}$. 48 is in between two perfect squares: 36, which is 6^2, and 49, which is 7^2. Note that 48 is very close to 7^2. Therefore, a reasonable estimate for $\sqrt{48}$ is 6.9.

17. **$5\sqrt{6} - 5\sqrt{2}$:** $\sqrt{150} - \sqrt{50} = (\sqrt{25} \times \sqrt{6}) - (\sqrt{25} \times \sqrt{2}) = 5\sqrt{6} - 5\sqrt{2}$

18. **$\sqrt{6}$:** $\sqrt{150} - \sqrt{96} = (\sqrt{25} \times \sqrt{6}) - (\sqrt{16} \times \sqrt{6}) = 5\sqrt{6} - 4\sqrt{6} = \sqrt{6}$.

19. **x^2:** $\sqrt{x^4} = x^2$. Note that we do not need to restrict x to non-negative values, because both x^4 and x^2 are always non-negative.

20. **$3\sqrt{5}$:** $\sqrt{20(4) - 5(7)} = \sqrt{45} = \sqrt{9} \times \sqrt{5} = 3\sqrt{5}$

21. **$3\sqrt{a}$:** Notice that we have two terms under the radical that both contain a. We can add like terms together if they are under the same radical: $\sqrt{2a + 7a} = \sqrt{9a}$. Now factor out and isolate squares under their own radical sign so that you can take their square root: $\sqrt{9a} = \sqrt{9} \times \sqrt{a} = 3\sqrt{a}$.

22. **$5^{\frac{1}{12}}$ or $\sqrt[12]{5}$:** $\sqrt[3]{\sqrt[4]{5}} = \sqrt[3]{5^{\frac{1}{4}}} = \left(5^{\frac{1}{4}}\right)^{\frac{1}{3}} = 5^{\frac{1}{12}} = \sqrt[12]{5}$

23. **2:** $\dfrac{\sqrt[4]{64}}{\sqrt[4]{4}} = \sqrt[4]{\dfrac{64}{4}} = \sqrt[4]{16} = 2$

24. $\sqrt{x+1} - \sqrt{x}$: For this problem, we need to multiply the numerator and denominator by the conjugate of the denominator. The conjugate is $\sqrt{x} - \sqrt{x+1}$:

$$\dfrac{1}{\left(\sqrt{x} + \sqrt{x+1}\right)} \cdot \dfrac{\left(\sqrt{x} - \sqrt{x+1}\right)}{\left(\sqrt{x} - \sqrt{x+1}\right)} = \dfrac{\left(\sqrt{x} - \sqrt{x+1}\right)}{x - \left(\sqrt{x}\right)\left(\sqrt{x+1}\right) + \left(\sqrt{x}\right)\left(\sqrt{x+1}\right) - (x+1)} =$$

$$\dfrac{\left(\sqrt{x} - \sqrt{x+1}\right)}{x - (x+1)} = \dfrac{\left(\sqrt{x} - \sqrt{x+1}\right)}{-1} = -\left(\sqrt{x} - \sqrt{x+1}\right) = \sqrt{x+1} - \sqrt{x}$$

25. **$32 - 12\sqrt{7}$:** For this problem, we need to multiply the numerator and denominator by the conjugate of the denominator. The conjugate is $8 - 3\sqrt{7}$:

$$\dfrac{4}{\left(8 + 3\sqrt{7}\right)} \cdot \dfrac{\left(8 - 3\sqrt{7}\right)}{\left(8 - 3\sqrt{7}\right)} = \dfrac{32 - 12\sqrt{7}}{64 - (8)(3)\sqrt{7} + (8)(3)\sqrt{7} - 3^2 \cdot 7} = \dfrac{32 - 12\sqrt{7}}{64 - 63} = 32 - 12\sqrt{7}$$

26. **(D)** $-17 - 8\sqrt{5}$: In order to simplify a fraction that has a difference involving a square root in the denominator, we need to multiply the numerator and denominator by the sum of the same terms (this is also known as the "conjugate"):

$$\frac{6+\sqrt{5}}{2-\sqrt{5}} = \frac{6+\sqrt{5}}{2-\sqrt{5}} \times \frac{2+\sqrt{5}}{2+\sqrt{5}} = \frac{(6+\sqrt{5})(2+\sqrt{5})}{2^2 - (\sqrt{5})^2} = \frac{12+2\sqrt{5}+6\sqrt{5}+5}{4-5} = \frac{17+8\sqrt{5}}{-1} = -17 - 8\sqrt{5}$$

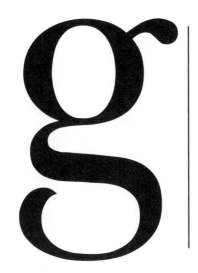

Chapter 13
of
NUMBER PROPERTIES

OFFICIAL GUIDE
PROBLEM SETS:
PART II

In This Chapter . . .

- Number Properties Problem Solving List
  from *The Official Guides:* PART II
- Number Properties Data Sufficiency List
  from *The Official Guides:* PART II

Practicing with REAL GMAT Problems

Now that you have completed Part II of NUMBER PROPERTIES it is time to test your skills on problems that have actually appeared on real GMAT exams over the past several years.

The problem sets that follow are composed of questions from three books published by the Graduate Management Admission Council® (the organization that develops the official GMAT exam):

The Official Guide for GMAT Review, 12th Edition
The Official Guide for GMAT Quantitative Review
The Official Guide for GMAT Quantitative Review, 2nd Edition
Note: The two editions of the Quant Review book largely overlap. Use one OR the other.

These books contain quantitative questions that have appeared on past official GMAT exams. (The questions contained therein are the property of The Graduate Management Admission Council, which is not affiliated in any way with Manhattan GMAT.)

Although the questions in the Official Guides have been "retired" (they will not appear on future official GMAT exams), they are great practice questions.

In order to help you practice effectively, we have categorized every problem in The Official Guides by topic and subtopic. On the following pages, you will find two categorized lists:

(1) **Problem Solving:** Lists MORE DIFFICULT Problem Solving Number Properties questions contained in *The Official Guides* and categorizes them by subtopic.

(2) **Data Sufficiency:** Lists MORE DIFFICULT Data Sufficiency Number Properties questions contained in *The Official Guides* and categorizes them by subtopic.

Remember that Chapter 9 in Part I of this book contains the first sets of Official Guide problems, which are easier.

Each book in Manhattan GMAT's 8-book strategy series contains its own *Official Guide* lists that pertain to the specific topic of that particular book. If you complete all the practice problems contained on the *Official Guide* lists in each of the 8 Manhattan GMAT strategy books, you will have completed every single question published in *The Official Guides*.

Problem Solving: Part II

from *The Official Guide for GMAT Review, 12ᵗʰ Edition* (pages 20–23 & 152–185), *The Official Guide for GMAT Quantitative Review* (pages 62–85), and *The Official Guide for GMAT Quantitative Review, 2nd Edition* (pages 62–86).

Note: The two editions of the Quant Review book largely overlap. Use one OR the other.

Solve each of the following problems in a notebook, making sure to demonstrate how you arrived at each answer by showing all of your work and computations. If you get stuck on a problem, look back at the NUMBER PROPERTIES strategies and content contained in this guide to assist you.

Note: Problem numbers preceded by "D" refer to questions in the Diagnostic Test chapter of *The Official Guide for GMAT Review, 12ᵗʰ Edition* (pages 20–23).

ADVANCED SET – NUMBER PROPERTIES
This set picks up from where the General Set in Part I leaves off.

Divisibility & Primes
> *12ᵗʰ Edition*: 106, 142, 198, 217, D13, D15
> *Quantitative Review*: 125, 164, 169 OR *2nd Edition*: 68, 112, 125, 149, 164, 169

Odds & Evens
> *12ᵗʰ Edition*: 185
> *Quantitative Review*: 150 OR *2nd Edition*: 152

Positives & Negatives
> *QR 2nd Edition*: 152

Consecutive Integers
> *12ᵗʰ Edition*: 201, 219, 224
> *Quantitative Review*: 160

Exponents & Roots
> *12ᵗʰ Edition*: 117, 137, 216, 230
> *Quantitative Review*: 149, 152, 163, 170 OR *2nd Edition*: 108, 147, 163, 170

CHALLENGE SHORT SET – NUMBER PROPERTIES
This set covers Number Properties problems from each of the content areas, including both easier and harder problems, but with a focus on harder problems. The Challenge Short Set duplicates problems from the General Set (in Part I) and the Advanced Set above.

> *12ᵗʰ Edition*: 36, 50, 82, 85, 106, 110, 116, 117, 137, 142, 157, 164, 216, 217, 219, 230, D13
> *Quantitative Review*: 103, 117, 122, 125, 145, 147, 149, 152, 160, 169, 170
> OR *2nd Edition*: 68, 86, 108, 112, 117, 122, 125, 147, 152, 169, 170

Data Sufficiency: Part II

from *The Official Guide for GMAT Review, 12th Edition* (pages 24–26 & 272–288), *The Official Guide for GMAT Quantitative Review* (pages 149–157), and *The Official Guide for GMAT Quantitative Review, 2nd Edition* (pages 152–163).

Note: The two editions of the Quant Review book largely overlap. Use one OR the other.

Solve each of the following problems in a notebook, making sure to demonstrate how you arrived at each answer by showing all of your work and computations. If you get stuck on a problem, look back at the NUMBER PROPERTIES strategies and content contained in this guide to assist you.

Practice REPHRASING both the questions and the statements. The majority of data sufficiency problems can be rephrased; however, if you have difficulty rephrasing a problem, try testing numbers to solve it. It is especially important that you familiarize yourself with the directions for data sufficiency problems, and that you memorize the 5 fixed answer choices that accompany all data sufficiency problems.

Note: Problem numbers preceded by "D" refer to questions in the Diagnostic Test chapter of *The Official Guide for GMAT Review, 12th Edition* (pages 24–26).

ADVANCED SET – NUMBER PROPERTIES

This set picks up from where the General Set in Part I leaves off.

Divisibility & Primes
> *12th Edition*: 98, 128, 171
> *Quantitative Review*: 83, 86, 88, 100, 110 OR *2nd Edition*: 82, 87, 90, 92, 115

Odds & Evens
> *12th Edition*: 106, 172

Positives & Negatives
> *12th Edition*: D41
> *Quantitative Review*: 111

Consecutive Integers
> *12th Edition*: 170
> *Quantitative Review*: 82 OR *2nd Edition*: 86

Exponents & Roots
> *12th Edition*: 166
> *Quantitative Review*: 106, 108, 116 OR *2nd Edition*: 31, 79, 110, 113

CHALLENGE SHORT SET – NUMBER PROPERTIES

This set covers number properties problems from each of the content areas, including both easier and harder problems, but with a focus on harder problems. The Short Set duplicates problems from the General Set (in Part I) and the Advanced Set above.

> *12th Edition*: 76, 82, 90, 106, 128, 159, 166, 170, 171, 172
> *Quantitative Review*: 3, 45, 53, 63, 75, 78, 82, 83, 86, 108, 110, 111, 116
> OR *2nd Edition*: 3, 31, 45, 54, 64, 78, 79, 81, 82, 86, 87, 90, 113, 115

mba Mission

Every candidate has a unique story to tell.

We have the creative experience to help you tell yours.

We are **mbaMission**, published authors with elite MBA experience who will work with you one-on-one to craft complete applications that will force the admissions committees to take notice. Benefit from straightforward guidance and personal mentorship as you define your unique attributes and reveal them to the admissions committees via a story only you can tell.

We will guide you through our "Complete Start to Finish Process":

- ☑ Candidate assessment, application strategy and program selection
- ☑ Brainstorming and selection of essay topics
- ☑ Outlining and essay structuring
- ☑ Unlimited essay editing
- ☑ Letter of recommendation advice
- ☑ Resume construction and review
- ☑ Interview preparation, mock interviews and feedback
- ☑ Post-acceptance and scholarship counseling

Monday Morning Essay Tip: Overrepresenting Your Overrepresentation

Many in the MBA application pool—particularly male investment bankers—worry that they are overrepresented. While you cannot change your work history, you can change the way you introduce yourself to admissions committees. Consider the following examples:

Example 1: "As an investment banking analyst at Bank of America, I am responsible for creating Excel models…."
Example 2: "At 5:30 pm, I could rest easy. The deadline for all other offers had passed. At that point, I knew…."

In the first example, the candidate starts off by mistakenly introducing the reader to the very over-representation that he/she should be trying to avoid emphasizing. In the second example, the banker immerses the reader in an unraveling mystery. This keeps the reader intrigued and focused on the applicant's story and actions rather than making the specific job title and responsibilities the center of the text. While each applicant's personal situation is different, every candidate can approach his/her story so as to mitigate the effects of overrepresentation.

To schedule a free consultation and read more than fifty Monday Morning Essay Tips, please visit our website:
www.mbamission.com